Grace,

Thanks for taking
a risk! You are
making a difference.

Lenora '99

The Diversity Advantage

A Guide to Making Diversity Work

The Diversity Advantage

A Guide to Making Diversity Work

Lenora Billings-Harris, CSP

Oakhill Press

Greensboro, North Carolina

This publication is designed to provide accurate and authoritative information in regard to the subject matter covered. It is sold with the understanding that the publisher is not engaged in rendering legal, accounting, or other professional service. If legal advice or other expert assistance is required, the services of a competent professional person should be sought. *From a Declaration of Principles jointly adopted by a committee of the American Bar Association and a committee of Publishers.*

10 9 8 7 6 5 4 3 2 1

Library of Congress Cataloging in Publication Data

Billings-Harris, Lenora, 1950–
    The diversity advantage : a guide to making diversity work /
Lenora Billings-Harris.
        p.   cm.
    Includes bibliographical references and index.
    ISBN 1-886939-25-X (hardcover   :   alk. paper)
    1. Diversity in the workplace.   I. Title.
HF5549.5.M5B52   1998
658.3 ' 008 -- dc21   98-9576
                                                                                              CIP

Oakhill Press
3400 Willow Grove Court
Greensboro, NC 27410-8600
Printed in the United States of America

To

My grandparents,
Wendell and Alice,
who helped me learn
how to give and
receive unconditional love.

My father and stepmother,
Sonny and Trudy,
who taught me
the importance
of independence.

My mother, Lois, whose
spirit gives me courage.

My husband and best friend,
Charles, who helps me
be all that I can be.

Contents

Acknowledgments

There are many people I would like to thank for their contributions and support in helping this book idea become a reality. Because of the sensitive topic, many who contributed their experiences remain nameless on the following pages. I thank the hundreds of seminar participants who were willing to share their stories and their pain so others could understand the importance of the subject of valuing diversity.

Thank you to the staff of Oakhill Press for providing such professional assistance at every step of the process.

I thank Courtney Schmidt and Karen Ahrens for their research and administrative support.

Without the constant support and unselfish guidance from the experienced authors who are members of the National Speakers Association, I never would have believed in myself as an author. Special thanks to Tracy Brown, Ed Scannell, Roger Herman, Joyce Gioia, and Margo Chevers.

1

What Is Diversity in the Workplace?

> **"Diversity:**
> **The art of thinking independently together."**
> —Malcolm Forbes

R obert, Faheem, Tracee, Kewal, Lois, Hernando, and
Dorothy are account executives for a small but rapid-
ly growing company. Their ages range from 23 to 59 years
old; two are single, two are married; three have life partners;
three are child-free, three are parents; one is gay and one is
blind; one is caring for a parent and two children; two are
single parents. There are four languages and six religions
represented by this group. This is diversity in the workplace.

The word *diversity* simply means differences or variety.
As used when referring to the American workplace, diversity
refers to the many differences present among workers today.
Diversity in the workplace includes all of the ways people are
different, not only differences in ethnicity, age, gender, and
ability so often thought of as part of EEOC (Equal Employment Opportunity Commission) regulations.

According to *Workforce 2000*, a research report published
by the Hudson Institute in 1987, 83% of new entrants into the
labor market will be other than able-bodied, white males by
the year 2000. The report also projected that 50% of the labor
market will be 50 years old or older. By the year 2050, 47%
of all Americans will be other than European American
(White). These shifts in demographics have already begun to
show themselves within the workplace, in the marketplace,
and in communities across the United States. The Hudson Institute's follow up report, *Workforce 2020,* 1997, substanti-
ates what it predicted in 1987, and it reemphasized the aging
of America.

The diversity movement as we know it today began in
earnest due to the above projections as well as several others
included in the Hudson Institute's *Workforce 2000* report.
Progressive organizations recognized that their employees of
the future would have different needs, expectations, and values than those possessed by the leaders of the company.

In order to attract the best talent, companies began to
evaluate their culture, their norms, and their expectations
with regard to acculturating people who are different. In

addition to the workplace looking different, another startling statistic was revealed originally in the *Workforce 2000* report. The labor market would be considerably smaller than it had been in the past (labor market = new entrants into the work-force). Because baby boomers did not have many children, there simply are fewer people available to work today. Com-panies are already experiencing huge competition for attract-ing the best talent.

These demographics present opportunities and chal-lenges. Since 1987, many organizations have gone through downsizing, right-sizing, re-engineering, and other eu-phemistic terms for terminating employees. Thus, those who remain often feel there is not enough time, not enough re-sources, and too much work to do per employee. This added level of stress, compounded by getting things done through working in teams, has created more opportunity for diversity collisions. Too often, organizations have grouped people to-gether and called them a team, when in fact they are still sim-ply a group of individuals, not a team working together.

Once individuals learn to respect differences of others, the work teams become more highly productive and innova-tive, and they often make fewer costly mistakes. A diverse workforce can assist organizations in their efforts to pene-trate emerging markets, attract and retain the best talent, im-prove customer relations, and reduce employee complaints and grievances. All of these challenges and opportunities have strong bottom-line implications.

Organizations that have taken the initiative to include di-versity as one of their business focuses have developed many diversity definitions and mission statements. As a basis for discussion throughout this book, I will use the fol-lowing definitions:

Valuing Workforce Diversity: Having the willingness and the ability to recognize, understand, respect, and utilize the contributions of all individuals, regardless of their packaging.

Managing Diversity: Having the ability and willingness to create and sustain an environment of respect, where all employees can reach their highest level of productivity, thus contributing to the success of the organization.

As you read this book continue to ask yourself, "How does the diverse environment affect me?" Allow yourself to explore its advantages and tackle personal challenges.

Making a Difference

1. **What have you noticed in your community and your workplace that reflects a growing change in demographics?**

   ❏ Multilingual voting ballots.
   ❏ Discounts for seniors.
   ❏ Two-income families.
   ❏ Single parents.
   ❏ Home-based businesses.
   ❏ Assigned parking slots for the physically challenged.
   ❏ TV programming varied rather than having stereotypical roles for certain actors.
   ❏ Women present in all types of positions. (There is really no such thing as a non-traditional job anymore for women or men.)
   ❏ People with disabilities more visible in all walks of life.
   ❏ Concern for political correctness.
   ❏ A variety of ethnic restaurants available.
   ❏ Telecommuting.
   ❏ More variety in the types of places of worship available.
   ❏ List others:

   _____

   _____

_____

_____

_____

_____

2. What challenges have these changes caused for you?

_____

_____

_____

_____

_____

3. What benefits have you observed or experienced as a result of diversity in your community and workplace?

_____

_____

_____

_____

_____

2

Why Should I Care about Diversity? How Does It Affect My Job Day to Day?

"Every effort for progress, for enlightenment, for science, for religion, for political, for economic liberty emanates from the minority, not from the masses."
—Emma Goldman

Have you ever had a clash with one of your staff members? Have any of your staff avoided or complained about working with another team member?

Most of the clashes or *diversity collisions* that happen at work occur because the individuals involved are unable or unwilling to recognize and value differences. The natural inclination is to judge differences. When a reason for the conflict cannot be readily identified, stereotypical beliefs or biases are often used to rationalize the cause.

Imagine that you supervise Wendell, who is a European American man, and Fatima, who is an African American woman. Both Fatima and Wendell have great ideas regarding ways to improve customer relations. They each, separately, have shared some of their ideas with you. Given that you want your employees to work well together in teams, you decide to assign the two of them to work together on a special project. Their assignment is to identify ways to improve customer service and develop an implementation plan. What you don't know is that Wendell and Fatima don't get along very well. Here's what could happen.

The report is due next Monday. It is now Wednesday. Because neither employee really wants to be around the other, they procrastinate until Friday. Finally, Fatima goes to Wendell's workstation to begin brainstorming this project. Every idea that Wendell shares, Fatima criticizes. Each time Fatima begins to share an idea, Wendell interrupts her. This behavior continues for 15 or 20 minutes. If these two adults were thinking logically and were really interested in solving this conflict, one or the other would eventually stop this interaction and analyze the process to determine how to improve it. Wendell might say, "Fatima, I appreciate that you so easily see the negatives in ideas. This can, sometimes, be beneficial because it helps people avoid errors. I would appreciate it, however, if you would look for the positives in my ideas as well."

Fatima, if she were thinking logically, might say to Wendell, "Please, let me complete my statements before you respond.

When you interrupt, I find it difficult to continue my train of thought in a non-defensive manner."

In other words, each individual would develop a contract with the other and come to agreement on how best to work with each other in order to complete the project. This type of positive conflict resolution rarely ever happens in the workplace. Everyone is already under stress due to lack of resources, lack of time, and sometimes lack of skill in dealing with these types of issues.

The two of them decide to meet on Monday morning. As they each get in their car to drive home, they could have the following thoughts:

Wendell is talking to himself in anger. "Why do I have to work with Fatima? She's a pushy, Black broad who thinks she knows everything. She's always on the defensive and she's probably suffering from PMS." Now, of course, all of Wendell's thoughts are stereotypical. It is possible that they could be true when applied to Fatima, but more likely he isn't talking about Fatima as an individual at all. The stereotypes are simply an easy excuse for the reasons they are ineffective when working together.

Fatima is driving home as well and her thoughts are no better. She says to herself, "This will never work. I'll never be able to complete this project successfully with Wendell. After all, he's a middle-aged, White guy. Certainly, he cannot deal with an assertive, professional Black woman such as myself. Plus, men never listen to women anyway. They're always interrupting. If it's not their idea, it's not a good idea." Fatima relies on stereotypes to generalize and rationalize why she is having a conflict with Wendell.

Monday morning they must meet again because they have not completed the project. They suffer through this process and eventually create a two- or three-page report for you. Is it their best work? That's doubtful. Has their productivity been affected? Of course. Have they resolved the conflict? No. Their stereotypes are based on past messages received over their lifetime, and perhaps a few direct experiences.

The stereotypes were just waiting in the background to be snatched up and applied to the first conflict situation. As you read this tale, you might say to yourself, "I just don't think that way." However, remember that you are probably in your logical state of mind at this moment, as you are reading this book.

Stereotypes tend to surface when you are stressed, afraid, or otherwise emotionally distressed. Most people rely on stereotypes, although it is often unconscious, because it is easier than resolving the conflict, and those chosen seem to fit.

Diversity affects you, with each encounter with another person. You are a culture of one; there is no one else just like you. Your differences or uniqueness can add to the strength of the organization if the environment is one that encourages recognition of differences and supports strategies and techniques to build on those differences in a harmonious way.

Making a Difference

1. **Think of someone with whom you have a conflict. What specific behaviors does this person act out that affect you negatively?**

_____

_____

_____

_____

_____

2. **List everything the two of you have in common.**

_____

_____

_____

_____

_____

_____

3. In what ways are the two of you very different? Include such things as age, ethnicity, gender, title, work location or department, education, and so on.

_____

_____

_____

_____

_____

4. Is it possible that stereotypical beliefs or biases are creating barriers to your effectiveness? (Be brutally honest. No one will see this except you.)

_____

_____

_____

_____

_____

5. **Identify the positive attributes of this individual. How can these attributes make your team stronger?**

_____

_____

_____

_____

_____

_____

6. **Take the first step. Have a conversation with this individual to resolve the conflict. (See chapter 16 to learn how to give feedback in a negative situation.)**

3

What Is the Difference Between Diversity and EEO/Affirmative Action?

"You can only protect your liberties in this world by protecting the other man's freedom. You can only be free if I am free."
—Clarence Darrow

During the past decade, many organizations have re-named their Affirmative Action efforts "diversity initiatives." This has often been a mistake. Although EEO and Affirmative Action are connected in their focus on inclusiveness, they are very different in their reason for existence. Because people have developed strong opinions about Affirmative Action and its usefulness, renaming these efforts *diversity* has made many people immediately oppose the initiatives.

Affirmative Action regulations require that an organization develop goals for hiring and promoting people who are within "protected classes." However, many people within the organization see these goals as quotas. Quotas are perceived as "ceilings"; when we achieve the quota, we can stop. Goals are perceived as "floors"; when we achieve a goal, we set a higher one.

Let's take a look at each of the three elements: Equal Employment Opportunity, Affirmative Action, and diversity.

EEO/AA	Diversity
• Civil Rights Act of 1964 • Executive Order 11246 (AA) • "Protected classes" • Federal regulations • Americans with Disabilities Act, 1990	• 1987—*Workforce 2000* • 1997—*Workforce 2020* • 83% of the new labor pool will be other than White males • No protected classes • Driven by business (proactive), not governmental force
Assumptions • "They" will conform to the mainstream to fit in (assimilate). • Ignore differences • "The USA is a melting pot"	***Assumptions*** • Notice and respect differences • Differences cultivate innovative teams • Acculturate instead of assimilate • "The USA is a tossed salad"

Equal Employment Opportunity:

Equal Employment Opportunity (EEO) refers to government-mandated regulations targeted toward organizations with 15 or more employees, "who engage in industries that affect commerce." These regulations were introduced as part of Title VII of the Civil Rights Act of 1964, which originally focused its efforts on creating opportunities in the workplace primarily for African Americans and women. "Protected classes" include people of color; women; people with disabilities (Americans with Disabilities Act of 1990); Vietnam War veterans; individuals of a religion, age, national origin; and others. In reality, everyone is protected under this act. Otherwise there would be no such thing as reverse discrimination. The primary focus of EEO has been to create equal hiring, development, and promotion opportunities for those who, in the past, were discriminated against because of the cultural group of which they were a member.

These regulations require that employers provide an *equal opportunity* for "protected class" individuals to apply for positions and an equal chance to be considered for promotion. For example, soon after the regulations were introduced, employers discontinued the practice of identifying jobs as "for women" or "for men" in the classified section of the newspaper. Theoretically job applications from people in the protected classes would be accepted by employers and considered equally along with those of European American males. Unfortunately, change was slow. Thus, Affirmative Action was introduced as a result of Presidential Executive Order 11246, signed by Lyndon B. Johnson in 1965.

Affirmative Action:

Affirmative Action (AA) requires businesses to create and maintain a workforce whose demographics match the community within which the business is located. If this is not the case, organizations are required to develop Affirmative Action plans that specifically identify what steps will be taken, yearly, to attract underrepresented people to the organization. Many companies became more visible as recruiters on campuses of HBCU's (Historically Black Colleges and Universities) placed ads in ethnic newspapers and magazines and became supporters of nonprofit organizations, such as the Urban League, in order to meet the requirements of Affirmative Action regulations.

The general assumption was that if enough "different" people worked together on a daily basis, racism, sexism, ageism, and the like, would eventually disappear from American society. It has not worked even though many people were, and are, allowed to work within organizations that would not have opened their doors otherwise without this government intervention.

Little or no attention had been given to how people were treated once they were hired. It was expected that once given the opportunity to join the organization, people were to assimilate themselves into the organization's norms, values, and behaviors, even if that meant they must deny their own cultural strengths. They were expected to sacrifice their individuality as it related to difference from the majority (i.e., ethnicity, gender, religion, etc.) and act as much like those in power as possible, if they expected to get ahead.

From the mid-70's through the mid-80's, in order to succeed in the corporate world, for example, women knew they should dress as much like men as possible. Many wore bow ties, dark suits, white blouses, and conservative jewelry, and cut their hair or pulled it back so it did not touch their shoulders. Corporate rationale was if women dressed in a feminine way, they would be too distracting on the job. It did not work. Men still noticed that women were women. More important, women should not have been held accountable for men's behavior. Although many women choose to dress very conservatively today, most progressive organizations recognize that attire does not, by itself, predict talent or potential. Additionally, the male uniform of dark suit, white shirt, and clean-shaven face has begun to fade as required attire for many jobs. Casual days and business casual dress has become the norm in many organizations.

The United States has been referred to as a melting pot, which implied that individuals must give up their uniqueness and wear a facade in order to get ahead. The rule was that you should not flaunt your differences. A melting pot is like a stew that cooks a long time. In the end, the flavor might be good but you cannot identify the individual ingredients. Everything loses its original identity and its unique strength.

Diversity:

At about the same time businesses were realizing that they were spending a great deal of time and money recruiting women and minorities but doing a poor job of retaining them, the Hudson Institute published its study of the labor trends in the United States. The U.S. Department of Labor needed to determine what the demographics of the labor market would be by the year 2000 and commissioned this study.

It was the findings of this report, called *Workforce 2000,* coupled with the realization that putting people together who are different does not mean they will automatically work well together, that began the *diversity movement.*

As organizations began to implement diversity initiatives, their motivations for actions were, and are, different than actions caused by EEO and Affirmative Action. Diversity initiatives are incorporated into the organization for one of three motivations:

1. It's believed to be the right thing to do by senior management.
2. The organization is losing money due to discrimination and sexual harassment lawsuits and/or high turnover.
3. Recognizing and respecting differences enables teams to be more highly productive.

Progressive organizations recognize that their worker demographics will be, and in many cases already are, very different than they were 20 or even 10 years ago. If businesses plan to be successful, they must start now to reexamine how they treat people, all people, employed within their company.

Because diversity initiatives are not a government mandate or regulation, there are no "protected classes." Businesses are motivated to initiate inclusive policies and practices because they foresee a bottom-line payoff. They are recognizing that the diversity of their employees adds to their strength in the marketplace. The more an organization "looks like" the market it serves, the more likely people will want to do business with them and work for them.

The values and expectations of organizational leadership are often very different than the values and expectations of the new worker. For example, many Generation X'ers and baby busters generally value quality of life issues more strongly than did baby boomers and Depression-era workers when they were young. Many choose where they plan to live first, then search for a job in that location, rather than moving to wherever the job is, as baby boomers and Depression-era adults did. It is no longer expected practice that within many organizations you must be ready to move your family every two years in order to succeed. Companies are finding innovative ways to retain talented, skilled workers because they run the risk of losing them to competitors if they ignore these important issues. Workers today are proud of their ethnic heritage and do not choose to hide or diminish it, as was expected in the past. Employees expect to be allowed to celebrate their religious holidays and wear religious attire to work.

Leaders today are confronted with these and other difficult issues unlike they ever had to consider before. Just as predicted in *Workforce 2000* and reconfirmed in *Workforce 2020,* the labor pool is shrinking. They wrestle with issues such as business casual attire, visible tattoos, and facial piercing as it relates to job performance because talent is scarce and it comes in all types of "packaging."

Thus, diversity celebrates differences instead of hiding or trying to change them. The more diverse a work team is, the more effective it can be if the team members respect each other's differences and value the contributions of those who are different. The challenge of leading a diverse organization is how to help workers feel valued and respected as individuals while helping everyone focus on the mission and goals of the organization.

When valuing diversity, the United States has been referred to as a "tossed salad" or "stir-fry." It has fruits and nuts along with vegetables, and each ingredient maintains its uniqueness while contributing to the overall flavor and value of the salad or stir-fry. The ingredients do not lose their identity in order to contribute.

Making a Difference

- To develop a deeper understanding of Equal Employment Opportunity and Affirmative Action, contact your local EEO office. Every city and state has such an office. It is this office that enforces the EEO and Affirmative Action regulations.
- To identify what diversity initiatives your company may have undertaken, contact your company's Human Resources Department. Discuss this with your manager and ask what initiatives are in place and how you can help support them.

Actions you can take to demonstrate your support of the *diversity advantage* within your work group:

- Mentor a new employee.
- Show intolerance of stereotypical comments, jokes, gestures, and the like.
- Evaluate others based on facts rather than judging based on bias or stereotypical beliefs.

4

What Are the Correct Terms and Why Must I Change My Words?

"Please don't say I'm 'wheelchair-bound' or even worse, 'confined' to a wheelchair."
—Rolf Hotchkiss

A re you tired of political correctness and wonder why it is suggested that language should become more sensitive? As our society and workplaces continue to expand their diversity, more and more people want to be referred to by terms they have chosen rather than the labels selected by others. Sometimes the power of words is underestimated. Thus, one ill-chosen word can create friction between people.

Many people with Latino heritage, for example, do not like the term *Hispanic* because it was a term formulated by the United States Census Bureau in 1970. When it was realized that many U.S. households consisted of families who spoke Spanish, there had not previously been a way to record this. Rather than attempt to identify every country from which these residents' ancestors might have come, the Census Bureau created the word *Hispanic*. Hispanic is not really an ethnic group. It is a generalized term used to describe a diverse group of people whose primary language is often Spanish.

On the other hand, some people of Latino heritage prefer the term *Hispanic* because they believe it carries less bias than the words *Mexican* or *Puerto Rican*, for example.

Many Blacks prefer *African American* because the word *black* is rarely capitalized, even when it is specifically referring to that ethnic group (except within books written by African Americans and magazines targeted to the African American culture), whereas *African American* does have the honor of capital letters. Some people believe the small case "b" is another example of subtle, institutionalized racism. African American is a term of pride. Unlike European Americans who can choose to recognize their Irish, German, or Italian heritage, African Americans do not have that option for recognizing their specific heritage. For many African Americans it is impossible to identify their ancestors' country of origin. On the other hand, some Blacks do not like *African American* because they see themselves as American and not African since Africa is not a country; it is a continent.

Each time I visit South Africa to work with organizations there, I am acutely aware that I am American, even though I am proud of my African heritage.

One person can never know all of the right words to use. However, when a reference must be made, ask people who are members of that group which term they prefer. The answers will vary. People have individual preferences, but your interest in asking questions will demonstrate your effort to show respect. Too often we assume, instead of asking, thus causing misunderstandings and conflicts. Perhaps a more effective way of referring to different ethnic groups is to place the word *American* in front of the ethnicity; for example, Americans of European heritage, Americans with Asian heritage, Americans with Latino heritage, and so on.

Although using words and phrases that show respect and sensitivity requires effort, it really is not very difficult or time-consuming. The following list highlights words and terms that can be substituted for the less respectful terms. Note that some phrases do not have a more acceptable alternative and should be eliminated from use altogether.

Insensitive Words and Phrases	Alternatives
• Black sheep	• Outcast
• "Guys" (when referring to a mixed group)	• Friends; folks; group
• Oriental (when referring to people)	• Asian (using the specific nationality, i.e., Korean, is even better, when possible)
• Acting like wild Indians	• Out of control
• Girls (when referring to co-workers)	• Women
• Policeman/postman	• Police officer/mail carrier
• Manhole	• Utility hole
• Chairman	• Chair
• Handicapped	• People with special needs; people who are physically/mentally challenged; people with disabilities
• Retarded	• Developmentally challenged
• Gifted children	• Advanced learners
• Race	• Ethnicity or nationality (there is only one race—human)
• Uneducated (when referring to adults)	• Lacking a formal education
• No culture (when referring to parts of the U.S. where the opera and the theater are scarce or nonexistent)	• Lacking European culture
• The little woman; the wife	• Your wife; his wife
• "Don't go postal on me!"	
• Acting blonde	
• Old people	• Seniors; chronologically advantaged
• Bitchy	• Assertive
• "White" lie	• Lie (calling it white does not make it okay)
• Flip chart	• Easel (flip is a derogatory word to Filipinos)
• Indian giver	
• Jew down	• Negotiate
• Half-breed	• Multi-ethnic
• Blacklisted	• Banned
• "Manning" the project	• Staffing the project

Making a Difference

It is impossible to constantly know what words show the most sensitivity, and when and how to use the most sensitive words all the time. Since "appropriate" words change all the time, try using the following suggestions:

- Ask several people within the same cultural group which terms they prefer.
- Omit slang terms when referring to others.
- Do not use derogatory terms to describe others even if people within the cultural group do. (For example, if a Jewish person tells a joke about Jews, that is not permission for others not in the group to do the same.)
- Refrain from joking about a person's bald head or lack of height. Even if the polite laugh, it does not mean they think it is funny.
- Lighten up, and show respect at the same time. Be willing to say, "I'm sorry," or "I didn't mean to offend." Most people will recognize your sincerity, if it is truly present.

5

How Can I Increase My Knowledge about Various Cultural Groups So That I Do Not Rely on Biased and Stereotyped Information?

"Bigotry is the child of ignorance and the parent of hostility."
—Anonymous

There are four cornerstones of diversity that, if developed, can help to create an inclusive, respectful, and productive working environment. (For information about the Discovering Diversity Profile, which measures these areas, contact Excel Development Systems Inc. toll free at 1-888-288-8885.) Each dimension requires personal action. However, they can be approached in any order.

The first cornerstone of diversity is knowledge. The diversity collisions that happen in the workplace are often accidental, unintended statements that are offensive or inappropriate. When knowledge is lacking, people will rely on the stereotypical or biased information gathered throughout a lifetime. Knowledge, in this context, is *the extent to which an individual possesses information about others from diverse backgrounds and cultures.* The more factual data that you have about other cultures and groups, the easier it is to be comfortable when interacting with people different than you. Use resources from films and videos, books, magazines, and the Internet (library, chat rooms, etc.) and talk to people within the group. Gathering information from these resources impacts our views and actions in relationship to people different than ourselves. The more accurate information we have about others, the more likely it is we will develop accurate opinions, feelings, and behaviors. Remember that you are only getting the perspective of that author, that director, that person, so it is important to use many different sources of information. The following is a list of possible resources for you.

Places and Events:

- Ethnic museums and memorials
- Historical societies
- Ethnic cooking classes
- Language classes
- Ethnic studies at colleges, universities, and libraries
- Different places of worship (mosques, synagogues, churches of different denominations, etc.)

- Participate in a pow wow
- Fine arts events
- Community theater
- Resources from government agencies (Human Rights Commission, Women's Commission, Equal Opportunity Offices, etc.)

Films:

This listing includes films based on actual history and films that identify attitudes, biases, and stereotypical thinking, even though the plots are fictitious. (Because there are so many films available, this list is not all-inclusive. If you are aware of others, this author would be happy to hear from you.) The letters after the names of the films indicate their subject matter: **D = disability**; **R = racism**; **S = sexual orientation**; **V = respecting differences** in general; **C = culture**; **A = age**.

A Class Divided	**R**
A Family Thing	**R**
Amistad	**R**
Awakenings	**D**
Babe	**V**
Birdcage	**S**
Braveheart	**R/C**
Cinderella (1997)	**V**
Cocoon	**A**
Dances with Wolves	**C**
Ghosts of Mississippi	**R**
Guess Who's Coming to Dinner	**R**
In and Out	**S**
La Familia	**C**
Mask	**D**
Mississippi Burning	**R**

Nell . . . . **D**
One Flew Over the Cuckoo's Nest . . . . **D**
Philadelphia . . . . **S**
Rainman . . . . **D**
Rising Sun . . . . **C**
Roots . . . . **R/C**
Rosewood . . . . **R**
Scent of a Woman . . . . **D**
Schindler's List . . . . **R**
Selina . . . . **C**
Sling Blade . . . . **D**
The Associate . . . . **V**
The Color Purple . . . . **R/C**
The Diary of Anne Frank . . . . **R/C**
The Diary of Miss Jane Pittman . . . . **R/C**
The Eye on the Prize . . . . **R/C**
The Joy Luck Club . . . . **C**
The Lion King . . . . **V**
The Shining . . . . **D**
To Kill a Mockingbird . . . . **R/D**

General:

- Public television programs
- The Internet (directories, libraries, chat rooms, bulletin boards, etc.) (See pages 131–134, Diversity on the World Wide Web.)

Magazines:

- *Black Enterprise*
- *Ebony*
- *Essence*
- *The Advocate*
- *10*
- *Latino*

- *Large Woman*
- *Working Woman*
- *Woman's World*

Books:
Genderflex, Judith Tingley, Ph.D.
Straight Talk About Gays in the Workplace, Liz Winfield
Proversity, Otis Graham
(See pages 129–130, Bibliography and Reference List, for others.)

Making a Difference

- **Rent a video about a group with whom you are reasonably unfamiliar. As you view it, notice the differences and similarities as compared to your own culture. Focus particularly on similarities and differences of:**
    - non-verbal massages
    - how respect is shown to authority
    - communication styles
    - concepts such as personal space, time, family, education
    - foods
    - traditions and rituals

- **Identify a group with whom you know you have a negative bias or attitude.**

- **Read a book or magazine about the group with the express purpose of identifying things they have in common with you.**

- **List in the space below the specific things you learned.**

_____

_____

_____

_____

The Four Cornerstones
of Diversity Development

Knowledge
—Stereotypes
—Information

Acceptance
—Tolerance
—Respect

Understanding
—Awareness
—Empathy

Behavior
—Self-awareness
—Interpersonal skills

The terminology "knowledge, understanding, acceptance, and behavior" was originally developed by Armida Russell, Amy Tolbert, Ph.D., and Frank Wilderman, Jr., Ph.D. as part of the Discovering Diversity Profile.

6

Some Stereotypes Are True, Aren't They?

"In Germany they first came for the Communists, and I didn't speak up because I was not a Communist. Then they came for the Jews, and I didn't speak up because I was not a Jew. Then they came for the trade unionists, and I didn't speak up because I was not a trade unionist. Then they came for the Catholics, and I didn't speak up because I was Protestant. Then they came for me—and by that time no one was left to speak up."

—Pastor Martin Niemoller

A stereotype is a generalized statement applied to everyone in the group, as though the entire group is the same. Any belief or characteristic, applied to an entire group, immediately makes it invalid because no characteristics are owned by everyone in the group.

Stereotypical beliefs do come from some degree of truth, however. There is probably someone in the group who fits the stereotype. The challenge is to acknowledge people as individuals without generalizing that individual's behaviors or characteristics. For example, a stereotype about African Americans is "Black people have rhythm." It is true that many African Americans are rhythmic. However, all African Americans do not have rhythm, and many people of other cultures do. In the movie, *White Men Can't Jump,* the title poked fun at the stereotype about European American men as though none of them could play basketball. Viewers of this movie have the opportunity to see that European Americans, otherwise known as white men, can jump.

There is no such thing as a "good" stereotype. All stereotypical beliefs lead to inaccurate assumptions about individuals, whether the belief is a positive one or not. In the United States, there is a widely held belief that Asian children are smart, especially in mathematics and science. It is true that many Asian American children test well in these subjects. However, they were not born smarter than other people. Their ability, as it relates to these two subjects, is a result of their environment. All Asian Americans are not highly intelligent in these areas, although many have grown up in a home environment that strongly supports education. If non-Asians were placed in a similar environment, they too could score well in math and science.

Here is an example of how even a *"good"* stereotype can be damaging.

Imagine you are observing a third-grade class. The class is composed of European American children except for three. One male child is a Latino. Another male child is an African

American, and the third child of difference is a Japanese American female.

This teacher is someone your parents are delighted to have in the school system. He is the type of individual that goes out of his way to help his students excel. He truly loves each child, spends his own money for additional resources, stays after school, and comes in early to be available to assist students in any way he can. In other words, his intentions are good. However, he is not aware of his own stereotypes. Therefore, he is not aware of how those stereotypes impact his behavior.

It's September, thus he does not yet know his students individually very well. As he plans his lesson, the teacher begins to determine which students he may need to spend additional time with in order that they too can perform well. He's going to teach long division. Which students do you think he will most likely conclude need additional assistance?

The next day he goes into class, teaches long division, and then distributes math problems to each student. He immediately walks over to the African American little boy. Now, remember, his intentions are good ones. He wants to help. Is it possible the African American male is doing well? Of course, yes, it is possible. Is it likely that this little student will, in some way, let the teacher know that he does not need help? That behavior is most unlikely. The teacher then walks over to the Latino student. Is it possible he too needs no assistance? It is unlikely that he will tell the teacher he does not need help.

The teacher never walks over to the Japanese American little girl, even though another stereotype in the United States is girls do not perform well in math and science. In this case the ethnic stereotype is stronger than the gender stereotype. Is it possible that the Japanese American little girl does need help? Of course, the answer is yes. Is it likely she will ask for help? Most likely, no. Even at eight years old, in the third grade, she probably knows from messages around her, in comic strips, from adults, and from peers, that she is supposed to be a good math student. Additionally, she may have learned from her culture never to ask a person in authority a question in public. This would imply that the person in authority was not clear, and could cause the authority figure to possibly "lose face."

Which students has the teacher's behavior impacted? I hope you would agree that all of the students have been negatively impacted. Certainly there would be some European American children who do need help. The teacher neglected them, while the African American and the Latino received unnecessary attention, which could have sent the wrong message to the other students.

As the children go to the playground, the teacher's behavior could now impact their behavior toward each other. Some students might assume that the Hispanic and the African American are teacher's pets and start a fight with them. Other students might assume that the Hispanic and African American must be slow learners because they get so much attention and start a fight with them.

If they continue to see the same or similar messages acted out, that teacher's behavior could impact their behavior later in life, when working with people who are different than they are ethnically.

It is impossible to get rid of stereotypes entirely. The best we can do is become more aware of our own stereotypes. This way we can become more aware of how our stereotypes impact our behavior. Becoming aware of stereotypes includes listening to that inner voice that quotes generalized statements, and then choosing not to act on those stereotypical beliefs. It takes a conscious effort to ignore them.

Making a Difference

- **Watch a television program or a movie, with a friend, with the specific intention of identifying all of the** stereotypical behaviors and statements. Discuss which biases and stereotypes you both observed and which ones you have believed and accepted for a long time.

Notes:

_____

_____

_____

_____

_____

- Ask someone you trust to alert you anytime you make a stereotypical comment. It is only with this feedback that you can become more aware of how often you may rely on your own stereotypes. Record what you have learned below:

_____

_____

_____

_____

_____

- When you recognize that you are having a communications conflict with someone, identify the many ways that person may be different than you. Perhaps their communication style is different. Perhaps their values are different. Or perhaps there are visible differences such as gender, ethnicity, or age. Set an objective to evaluate the specific interaction between yourself and that person. In other words, evaluate the facts instead of relying on stereotypes. Then discuss your findings with the individual in order to resolve the conflict.

7

How Do I Begin to Improve My Understanding of People Different Than Me?

"Respect…is appreciation for the separateness of the other person, of the ways she or he is unique."
—Annie Gottleib

U nderstanding is *the extent to which an individual comprehends how others feel and why they behave as they do* according to Tolbert, Mendez-Russell, and Wilderson. With enhanced awareness we begin to see how our personal reality may not be the only reality. Better awareness helps us understand how others feel. It clarifies who we are in comparison to others, and it gives us a basis for contrasting our own cultural viewpoints with those of other people.

Because of cultural differences, people may see the same situation differently. For instance, among the Navajo Nation there is not a direct way to say, "be on time," because time is relative. Things happen "when it is time." If you are doing something important with other people, being on time is not considered to be more important. In the mainstream European American business world, "time is money." Being on time, being punctual, is very important, regardless of what you may be doing with others.

During one of my seminars with an Arizona client, a participant explained how difficult it sometimes is to impart the significance of being on time when his group is working with some of the Native Americans on the reservation. This is not an example of right or wrong. This is an example of being different. He said there was a trainee who did not return to class for three days, and also did not call to explain the absence. When the student finally did return, his reason for being absent was that he had had a death in the family and had to attend a Pow Wow. Of course, this was much more important than going to class. Time is relative.

With an enhanced understanding of why people do what they do, we can become less quick to judge and more able to empathize. Empathy is the ability to make connections with others on an emotional level. People who are empathic and aware can comprehend the emotions others are experiencing. They tend to recognize the reasons for points of view held by people from diverse backgrounds. This goes beyond knowledge of facts.

There are many resources around you, right in your community, that can help enhance understanding and enable you to develop more empathy for diverse groups. The key is to explore many sources and, most important, to talk to people within the group about which you want to learn. As you talk to people, realize that they may not know all of the answers to your questions. When you grow up within a culture and practice its traditions, you may not necessarily know why the traditions are as they are.

While attending a recent National Speakers Association Convention, I had the opportunity to attend a Jewish worship service for the first time. I was so excited to have the opportunity. Having been raised a Baptist, I was curious about the traditions of the Jewish faith.

I quickly discovered that my friends, who were sitting next to me and who are Jewish, did not necessarily know why we were doing some of the wonderful activities that were included in the service. In contrast, many Christians practice traditions such as having an evergreen Christmas tree, lights on the tree, and giving gifts, yet they do not know why each of those traditions has become part of their religion.

As you plan your study, include religion, language, foods, music, and the arts. If you study or participate in any of these areas, you will develop a better appreciation for and understanding of diverse groups.

Religion includes many of the values of the culture. Language demonstrates the values and biases of various cultural groups. Ethnic food requires you to do more than just eat and enjoy the food. You need to research why certain foods have become staples for that particular ethnic group.

As an adult interested in this area, I discovered that my favorite vegetable, collard greens, which is considered "soul food," has a story connected to it. During the early slave days, the slave masters did not provide very much food at all for their slaves. Therefore, the African women searched through the undeveloped parts of the plantation—the woods and the forest—to see what might be growing that they recognized from Africa. They soon discovered that collard greens, salad greens, and other green leafy vegetables were growing wild on many of the Southern plantations. Since the slave owners did not eat these foods, the slaves were able to expand the amount of healthy food available to them.

All ethnic food has some story like this, connected to it, which can help you understand that culture a bit better.

The following is a list of places, events and activities that might be available in your local area. The more adventurous may choose to travel around the country and outside of the country to learn more about diverse groups.

- Ethnic museums and memorials
- Historic societies
- Ethnic cooking classes
- Language classes
- Ethnic studies at colleges, universities, and libraries, such as Asian American studies, African American studies, women's studies, and so on.
- Various places of worship, such as mosques, synagogues, churches of different denominations, the Bahai faith center, temples
- Pow Wows
- Fine arts events
- Women's shelters
- Homeless shelters
- Special Olympics
- Anytown, USA (1-800-283-Hugs)
- The Hispanic Women's Conference
- 100 Black Women Clubs
- Oktoberfest
- Greek festival
- Ethnic restaurants
- Rodeos

- Community theater
- The Human Rights Commission
- The Women's Commission

If you can think of others, list them here:

_____

_____

_____

_____

_____

_____

Making a Difference

Set a time and date to volunteer or visit one of the suggested resources. Make it a fun event. Go with friends, relatives, or your children. As you participate, notice what customs are different than your own and ask questions.

Describe your experiences and reactions below:

_____

_____

_____

_____

_____

_____

8

If I Accept the Beliefs and Behaviors of Some People, Does That Mean I Condone Them?

We don't see things as they are,
we see things as we are.
—Anaïs Nin

The immediate answer to this question is, No. To con-
done means to approve. Acceptance the way I use it,
as it relates to accepting others different than you, means
*having the willingness and ability to respect and value char-
acteristics, customs, and behaviors of others.* This does not
include inappropriate behavior, such as breaking the law or
harassing others. With acceptance we can become more
relaxed and tolerant of others.

By developing the ability to accept others, ultimately respect for each individual is established. Seeing value in having a diversity of viewpoints, even if they cause a debate, is
healthy and productive. The outcome can be a broadening of
understanding for all parties, even if they agree to disagree.
Think of your own family. Does everyone agree all the time?
Probably not, but hopefully everyone still accepts each other.
In the workplace, the strongest, most effective teams have a
diversity of viewpoints from many different types of people.
The decisions made by such a team then reflect the group's
best thinking, instead of just the ideas of the most powerful
member.

Acceptance manifests itself through our behavior in many
ways. This story illustrates the point. When I lived in Arizona,
my husband and I socialized with two other couples frequently. The six of us often went to dinner together, and we did
not always sit next to our life partner. One evening at Ayako's,
a fun Japanese restaurant, we experienced lack of acceptance.
The couple's combination was as follows: one White couple,
one African American couple, and one Bi-racial couple. Another couple, Pete and Diane, who were strangers to us, and
who happened to be White was seated at our table to enjoy the
chef's entertaining meal preparation. Since we were planning
to have great fun, we greeted the new couple immediately,
with the hopes that they would be comfortable talking to and
responding to the chef, as we intended to do.

As the evening wore on it became obvious, due to their
questions of us, that they were trying desperately to determine

who was married to whom, and why we were all together. To Diane and Pete the "ethnicity matchup" did not fit. There were two White women and one African American woman; two African American men and one White man. Since we were not sitting next to our mates, and only one couple wore wedding bands, this was puzzling Pete and Diane. They never asked directly who was with whom, but it was obvious that they were wondering.

Pete asked, "How did you become friends?" One of the guys responded, "We have just known each other a long time, and like to party together." As the meal ended, and all of us were leaving the restaurant, Diane said to me, "I got it! You all sell Amway, and you are in town for a rally!" Isn't it sad that she could not accept that we were friends *just because* and not because of anything in particular. When Pete saw us pair up finally, he seemed relieved to see that only one couple was Bi-racial.

When we are not willing to accept diversity as being normal, we look for all kinds of rationales.

Making a Difference

Developing acceptance requires you to "get out of your comfort zone." Broaden your view point by trying the following suggestions:

- Seek different points of view from friends and associates by discussing politics, religion, creationism versus evolution, right to life versus pro-choice, etc. Remember, it is okay to agree to disagree.
- Listen to children. Really listen. When adults do not intervene, often children show a refreshing point of view on many things.
- Become a volunteer for Big Brother/Big Sister in your community or another similar organization. In addition to being a role model for your little "sister" or "brother,"

you will learn many things about a real person who has a background different from yours.

- If you are a sales or customer service representative, intentionally sell to or serve a customer who represents a group you tend to be intolerant of or impatient with. Focus on being patient and asking questions for clarity. Be aware of your stereotypes, but do not act on them.

- Keep a journal or diary of your experiences.

As you explore and practice the suggestions listed in this section of each chapter, you will be developing the fourth cornerstone of diversity, "behavior," which is illustrated in the previous model on page 35.

9

I Realize Valuing Differences May Be the Right Thing to Do, But What's the Business Need?

"Everyone wants a voice in freedom—the freedom to express our individuality in work and life. That's a fire burning inside all of us."
—Lech Walesa

Before embarking on any diversity initiative, including Diversity Awareness Training, your organization should be clear about its purpose for doing so and the results it expects. The clients with whom I have worked generally embark upon diversity for one of three reasons:

1. In their leadership's mind, it is the right thing to do.
2. To avoid costly lawsuits.
3. To enhance organizational productivity and profitability.

It's the right thing to do.

A few years ago, the American Heart Association decided to embrace diversity at all levels. As a nonprofit organization that provides services to the public, their leadership realized that heart attacks do not discriminate. Therefore, their staff and volunteers needed to develop a fuller understanding of all potential clientele.

The American Heart Association's Diversity Initiative had several segments. We offered diversity training to their community outreach volunteers across the country; they analyzed their marketing materials to make them more inclusive; and we evaluated recruiting tactics to discover more and better ways to recruit volunteers from all ethnic groups and economic levels.

Planned Parenthood of Central and Northern Arizona recognized that its Board of Directors, in its makeup, did not reflect the communities the organization serves. The initiative started at the board level and then reached all employees within every clinic and its central offices.

Although both organizations embarked upon diversity because they believed it was the right thing to do, they both quickly recognized the bottom-line impact even though they are non-profits. With a higher focus on valuing differences, organizations are able to more easily recognize how they may have overlooked simple procedures that inhibit or prohibit prospective clients from utilizing their services. Clinic hours of operation and location sometimes prohibited American Indians living on a reservation from utilizing services. The board and staff had, in the past, wondered why their utilization numbers from American Indians were so low. Once they recognized this problem, they were able to change clinic hours and arranged to provide transportation for individuals needing consultations and health checkups.

From these examples you can quickly see that "doing the right thing" can lead to higher utilization of services, efficiency, and good business sense.

To avoid lawsuits and discrimination claims.

Although this motivation is negative and reactive rather than proactive, many diversity awareness classes have been conducted because organizations have suffered the consequences of insensitivity and/or direct discrimination. In November of 1996, Texaco settled a discrimination case out of court for over $17 million. No matter how large or small the company, paying money for inappropriate behavior in the workplace is a drain to the bottom line. It damages public image. It affects recruiting, retention, and productivity among all employees.

While many organizations have jumped on the "diversity bandwagon," many have chosen only to provide diversity training. This has been a mistake. With only training and no plans to truly evaluate systems and processes to be sure all individuals are respected, developed, and encouraged to reach their highest potential, frequently more misunderstandings erupt instead of fewer.

The types of discrimination and harassment claims appearing in court are quickly growing. The 1997–98 Supreme Court is about to hear a harassment case involving same-sex individuals. They will soon decide whether or not it is illegal for someone of the same gender to harass another person. Regardless of the outcome, all individuals should have the right to work in an environment that supports them as contributing employees, regardless of their gender, sexuality, or ethnicity. When I share information about various court cases or pending court cases with participants attending my seminars, many times someone will say, "That is just not fair." What they mean is it is not fair that people can be sued because of what they say or do in the workplace. We all have a right to our own opinions. The converse is, we all have a right to earn a living without fear of harassment or discrimination.

To enhance organizational productivity and profitability.

More and more organizations are recognizing that the real reason to embark upon any diversity initiative is to contribute to the success of the organization. By creating an environment that values diversity of all types and helps individuals feel included, the organization enhances its competitiveness in every way. Companies who embark upon diversity for this reason realize quickly that more than training will be necessary.

Sometimes difficult decisions must be made that challenge values and beliefs that were never discussed before in the workplace. For example, Disney and AT&T realized that to help all employees feel included and valued, they needed to recognize homosexual couples in their benefits plan as it relates to beneficiaries and health care. Making the decision to recognize homosexuals in that way prompted boycotts and negative publicity. Companies today must weigh the loss of business versus gain of potential business and the overall advantages and disadvantages of attacking diversity issues that make some people uncomfortable.

Diversity, therefore, should be addressed just as any other business issue would. By relating to the overall mission and vision of the organization, then analyzing business objectives, diversity initiatives will become much clearer. By evaluating all business issues, several companies have realized that creating a diverse workforce and supporting that workforce leads to the following benefits:

- Lower turnover and higher loyalty
- Reduced employee conflict and tension
- Improved morale
- More effective and innovative teams
- More objective, performance-based criteria used for performance evaluation
- Reduced training costs due to higher retention
- Better client relations
- Improved interdepartmental relations
- Better and more inclusive mentoring and coaching

Although diversity entails more than training, that is a good place to start to raise awareness. To make an effective difference, organizations should evaluate the organizational benefits of effectively managing diversity and clarify expected results to all concerned. I suggest that you follow the following six major stages.

Stage 1: Assess the need. Review the organization's business objectives, mission, and goals and determine which of them may be impacted by diversity in a positive or negative way. Conduct an organizational diversity assessment to determine possible issues and concerns surrounding diversity. (For further information on how to conduct a Baseline assessment, call Excel Development Systems, Inc. toll-free 1-888-288-8885.) Do not assume that the people responding to the survey understand what diversity is. Use other words to identify the issues you're targeting. Evaluate the organizational systems such as recruiting, compensation, performance management, and career development. Develop questions about leadership and the overall work environment. As part of the assessment, a diversity council or committee should develop *visual descriptors* to identify what the organization will be once it has achieved its goal of inclusiveness.

A *visual descriptor* is a sentence that describes what people would be saying and doing, and the general attitudes they would have, about the organization after the objective has been achieved.

One client developed visual descriptors for several areas of the business. The following are a few examples:

- Competitors will look to us for best practices in the industry.
- Competitors know the best talent wants to work for our organization.
- The leadership demographics reflect worker demographics.
- Employees will feel free to take risks to solve problems.
- Employees are proud to work for our company.
- Work teams are innovative.
- Employees know that our leadership listens and supports them.
- The community rewards our efforts as a good corporate citizen.
- We are financially successful.
- We have a strong market share.
- We are viewed as leaders, not followers, in our market.

Notice that this list does not focus on ethnicity and gender. When all workers feel valued and respected the resulting behavior of the organization demonstrates good management practices in general.

Stage 2: Analysis. Analyze the results of the assessment as they compare to business directives and objectives such as increasing market share, turnover, customer satisfaction, and so on. Once this has been completed, then it will become more evident which diversity directives are most urgent.

Stage 3: Awareness. Develop and deliver customized diversity awareness training to all involved, starting at the top. It is imperative that everyone understands why the company is focusing on diversity, what it means to the company, and how it affects each employee. The training produces an organizational baseline of understanding of the issues.

Stage 4: Evaluate business systems. The most effective

approach for evaluating organizational systems is to use one or several teams, often called diversity councils or diversity committees. These teams should have a very specific mission. For example, one team could study and address the perception of leadership; another, development and performance evaluation; another, customer service; another, hiring and retention; another, community relations; and another, general marketing. Each team would evaluate the organization's processes and procedures within a specific area and determine whether or not there are barriers or bridges to valuing diversity.

Stage 5: Evaluation and re-assessment. To determine if any progress is being made after diversity initiatives have been implemented, an evaluation is necessary. It can take the form of surveys, interviews, or focus groups. After analyzing the results of the evaluation, the next steps can be determined based on the results and your original assessment of business objectives.

Stage 6: Business results. As a separate evaluation, business results should be analyzed. It is critical to realize, however, that diversity initiatives take a long time to produce a measurable result. Therefore, visual descriptors should be evaluated.

Making a Difference

Within your department or work unit evaluate the following, and note your findings for future reference:

Hiring—Are many different types of people seriously considered for available positions, or are opportunities given only to people who look, act, and speak like the present staff?

Retention—When people with differences are hired (i.e., ethnicity, age, gender, communication style, educational level, etc.) is their length of tenure similar to that of others, or do they leave the organization sooner?

Marketing—Do the organization's marketing materials, annual report, and newsletters reflect the diversity of the workforce via photos, rewards, and feature articles?

Feedback—Are employees asked what they think about issues, and if so does leadership listen and take action when appropriate?

Six Stages of Diversity Success

1. Assess need.
- —Identify business objectives.
- —Benchmark best practices.
- —Determine business case for a diversity initiative.
  (Councils or task forces)

2. Analyze.
- —Conduct a baseline survey of employee perceptions regarding diversity issues.
- —Correlate results with business operational objectives.
- —Develop visual descriptors.
  (Company or department-wide)

3. Be Aware.
- —Educate the organization to create a base of understanding of the business need to embrace diversity.
  (Company or department-wide)

4. Evaluate and enhance business systems and processes.
- —Concurrent with awareness development, evaluate H.R. processes as well as marketing; community relations; product/service development; and so forth.
  (Task forces)

5. Reassess employee perceptions.
- —Resurvey employees and compare results to baseline.
- —Identify success and areas needing further focus.
- —Determine next steps.
  (Company or department-wide)

6. Evaluate business results.
- —Compare business results to visual descriptors.
- —Determine actions needed to make new behaviors part of the company culture.

10

In Today's Environment of Political Correctness, It's Too Difficult to Know What to Do. Isn't It Easier Just to Treat Everybody the Same?

> "A great coach doesn't try to change a great player. Instead, the coach discovers what is unique, what is great about each player—and then honors it, is happy for it, uses it."
> —John Bunn

Yes, it may appear to be easier to treat everyone the same. The reality is none of us treats everybody exactly the same way. What we really need to do is stop pretending that we treat everyone the same. If you have sisters and brothers, or sons and daughters, ask yourself, do you treat each of them exactly the same way? Do you treat each of your parents exactly the same way? Surely the answer is no. You interact with each individual based on that individual's personality, skills, interests, and so on. That behavior recognizes differences. We need to expand that understanding and that willingness to adapt to the workplace. In interacting with people this way, we are showing our unconditional acceptance. Although it takes effort, we can be accepting of others more frequently in the workplace if we consciously focus on doing so.

For years managers were taught to treat everybody the same. The intention in that message was to treat everyone fairly. Treating people fairly does not mean treating them the same. The most effective leaders create and enforce fair guidelines in the workplace. Yet they recognize the unique strengths and talents of individuals so that they can create an environment that motivates each individual to work toward his or her highest level of potential. Think of Phil Jackson, the coach of the Chicago Bulls. Do you suppose he coaches/manages Dennis Rodman exactly the same way that he coaches/manages Michael Jordan and Scottie Pippin? I doubt it. The best coaches identify the talent, determine the most motivating environment for that individual, create the environment, and get out of the way. In other words, they train and then empower the individual to do the best he or she can do.

This is definitely more difficult than treating everyone the same.

Many managers will say to me, "Well, I just use the Golden Rule. Treat other people the way I want to be treated and then I should be safe, right?" Wrong. All of us, regardless of our religious or spiritual upbringing, have learned some variation of the Golden Rule, treat other people the way you wish to be treated. When considering ethics and values, the Golden Rule does work. If I want you to be honest with me, I must be honest with you. However, when considering interpersonal relationships and general communication, the Golden Rule is completely ineffective, because it assumes that the other person wants to be treated the same way I want to be treated. That assumption is wrong most of the time.

From an ethics and values point of view, all of us want respect, all of us want opportunities that are fair. All of us want to earn enough money to meet and, perhaps, exceed our needs. Each of us, however, goes about those wants and needs differently. The most effective leaders pay close attention and provide the environment that best allows individuals to reach their objectives. Companies today are recognizing more and more that they must treat people differently, yet fairly, in order to provide this motivating environment. Issues such as childcare, elder care, adoption, male and female parental leave, flex time, job sharing, telecommuting, formalized mentoring, retirement training, and career development training are all being tackled by progressive organizations today. They realize that the more they can accommodate the needs of their workers, the more likely they will keep good people.

What this really means is that leaders today must consider not only the external, easily determined differences among their workers such as ethnicity, gender, age and job title, but they must also consider the differences in values and perspectives. Then they must determine a way to honor those differences while coordinating them with the vision, mission, goals, and objectives of the organization. Not an easy task but certainly one that is achievable if management is open to ideas and willing to listen.

Making a Difference

- Find out what the interests of your workforce are. There are many ways to gather this information.
- Conduct focus groups. Allow the senior manager to sit and listen and not give excuses for things not done in the past.
- Create a formal or "informal" mentoring program that includes people at all levels and includes mentoring non-management/technical positions as well as the more typical management positions.
- Learn what other companies are doing in your community or other competitors are doing to make their work environment more attractive to employees.
- Create innovation teams. They go by many names today: performance teams, drive teams, cross-functional teams, and so on. Assign each with a task to identify creative ways to improve productivity by valuing diversity.

11

I Am Puzzled . . . Let's Take a Break.

> **Learning is developing a new capacity to do something or think in a way you couldn't before.**
> —Peter Senge

If you have made it this far in the book, you deserve a break. Adults learn best when having a good time. Although the subject of diversity is a serious one, we don't have to take ourselves so seriously while in the learning process.

Below is a puzzle and a challenge. Most of the words contained in the puzzle are words considered to be inappropriate. Although political correctness is important, at times it is taken to levels of the absurd. Society often must go to extremes in the midst of change before it finds a happy medium. The clues fit this category. There are a few appropriate terms, just to keep you on your toes.

The challenge is to find the words that correlate with the clues. Break the unwritten rule of not writing in books. When you think you have found all of them, tear out this page and mail your answers to me to receive a prize (copies not accepted). You will receive the Discovering Diversity Profile (a $13.00 value) one of the most widely used statistically valid and reliable diversity profiles in the United States.

Mail your answers to:

Lenora Billings-Harris, CSP
Excel Development Systems, Inc.
PO Box 1628
Greensboro NC 27402

GOOD LUCK AND HAVE FUN!

Are you politically correct?

Fun, "politically correct" words and phrases

(Words are spelled without hyphens or spaces)

```
O  R  I  E  N  T  A  L  P  E  R  S  O  N  X
Y  U  Q  S  K  N  U  R  D  R  Q  J  P  D  S
Q  N  S  F  F  D  H  I  O  W  W  B  R  K  S
U  E  T  T  A  E  U  O  B  A  M  H  R  Z  K
Z  D  U  O  T  T  P  J  D  A  B  C  I  N  Q
E  U  P  T  S  F  U  J  P  L  K  A  R  T  J
L  C  I  D  Y  I  P  R  A  E  F  I  W  X  E
O  A  D  E  U  G  I  C  E  N  G  P  A  W  E
H  T  C  A  G  S  K  R  G  N  P  Y  O  F  M
N  E  M  D  O  L  U  S  I  I  Z  U  I  W  R
A  D  L  N  I  L  H  N  L  A  R  W  X  W  E
M  Z  E  S  I  E  N  Y  L  W  U  L  Z  D  P
H  R  T  A  R  A  H  O  M  E  L  E  S  S  A
Q  E  F  O  M  A  N  P  O  W  E  R  K  G  P
D  E  V  K  P  R  E  G  N  A  N  T  M  E  C
```

Incomplete success	Economically exploited
Melanin impoverished	Sobriety deprived
Utility hole	Processed tree carcasses
Terminally disadvantaged	Prewoman
Client of the correctional system	Domestic incarceration survivor
Possessing an alternative body image	Cerebrally challenged
Parasitically oppressed	Asian person
Advanced (learner)	Lacking formal education
Staffing	Banned
Slang for a mixed-gender group	Motivationally dispossessed
Insignificant other	Involuntary undomiciled
Human resources	Female hero

12

Isn't This a Free Country? Why Am I Not Free to Say What I Really Think at Work?

"The great companies and teams are those that celebrate the differences. They seek harmony not uniformity. They hire talent not color. They strive for oneness not sameness."
—Gil Atkinson

It is paradoxical that we live in a country that protects free speech so fiercely, yet some speech is considered inappropriate. The reality is that words do hurt. They do impact productivity in the workplace if repeated often.

In the past, many who were affected by hurtful, racist, sexist, or homophobic comments just said nothing. Often they left the company, only to discover that the unaccepting environment existed elsewhere. Today workers are not so willing to keep "grinning and bearing" inappropriate behavior in the workplace. Courts have upheld accusations of "a hostile environment." Often the offending person as well as the company must pay damages to the victim.

Ultimately, everyone wants to have the opportunity to contribute to their fullest degree possible in an environment that respects him or her. Showing respect includes taking responsibility for one's own actions and speaking up when inappropriate comments are made. The following poem demonstrates this point.

Who Am I?

Who am I?
I am the Latino teenager who works
part-time in your mailroom.
You know
The one you think is in a gang,
Just because I use street slang.

Who am I?
I'm the Black woman who works
in your group.
You know
The one who wears her hair in braids,
or a natural, or dreadlocks,
the one you call a radical with
an attitude.

Who am I?
I am your blind neighbor.
You know
The one you always speak loudly to,
as though I had a hearing disability,
instead of one of sightlessness.

Who am I?
I'm the Korean grocer in your
neighborhood.
You know
The one you call unfriendly, just
because I don't smile enough for you.

Who am I?
I am a lesbian, or the gay person
who is your associate.
You know . . . oops, maybe you don't know.
I chose not to share that aspect of
Who I am,
Because you and your friends are
always joking about "Homo's", and
"queers", and "lesbos".
If you only knew how closely I work with you.

Who am I?
I am the Japanese American who
works in your sales department.
You know
The one whose name you make fun of
and expect me to laugh.

Who am I?
I am the Christian woman who travels
with you to make client calls.
You know
The one you keep apologizing to,
every time you tell an off-color joke,
or use God's name in vain.
Why do you apologize?
You obviously are not sorry, or you would
change your behavior.

Who am I?
I am the older man.
You know
The one you get impatient with
because I don't talk, move, or drive
as fast as you do.
One day you will be old, unless
you experience the only other alternative.

Who am I?
I am your administrative assistant.
You know
The one you always call "Hon" or "Sweetie"
whenever you want coffee.
How many years will it take for you
to learn my real name?

Who am I?
I am the new associate who just
relocated to your office.
You know
The one you imitate all the time,
because of my southern accent.

Who am I?
I am the American Indian.
You know
The one you call chief, and ask how's my squaw.
If you were interested in me as an individual,
you would know
that squaw is a derogatory French Canadian term,
and chief is not a word I joke about.

Who am I?
I am the Puerto Rican.
You know
The one who speaks Spanish to my
friends at work.
You think we are talking about you . . .
Don't flatter yourself.

Who am I?
I'm the African American man who
works down the hall.
You know
the one you and your friends say,
I only got my job because of my
color, of course not because I was the
best candidate.

Who am I?
I am the Chinese American human
resource specialist.
You know
The one you keep asking to help you with your computer,
even though I don't understand that technical stuff either.

Who am I?
I am the European American man.
You know
The one you blame for the errors
made over 200 years ago,
the one you think "has it made",
the one you think "just doesn't get it",
even though I am your strongest
advocate among my peers.

Who am I?
I am an American person
I worry about the environment,
education for my children, my next
paycheck, crime, and crabgrass
in my front yard.
I am the person who wants to know
the real you, if only you would act
interested in the real me.

—Lenora Billings-Harris, 1994

Making A Difference

Listen to your inner voice. Really concentrate on the messages you hear throughout the day. Record below

    —the stereotypical judgements you make of others
    —The stereotypes you hear from others

_____

_____

_____

_____

_____

_____

Make a commitment to yourself. For the next seven days, do not accept stereotypes as truth. Tell your inner voice, "Thanks but no thanks," when it makes a stereotypical or biased statement, then serach for the facts. When someone else utters stereotypical comments, ask, in a polite way, "Why do you think that is so?" Sometimes just a question can raise awareness.

13

What Are the Offensive Statements People Say, Accidentally?

"It's time we stopped fighting over the size of the pie
and worked together to build a bigger pie."
—Cavett Robert

Have you ever wished you could change the behavior of others when they are referring to a group to which you belong? Often people say and do things without intending to be offensive, but the outcome is discomforting never the less. As a result of a group exercise I frequently use in diversity awareness workshops, many participants are enlightened by their associates regarding the pain caused by words and actions not usually intended to hurt. The lists below were developed by many small groups of people, who are members of the group being discussed.

You may see contradictions within lists. Remember, everyone is unique, and has the right to their own opinion. I share this to help you identify the words, actions, and stereotypes that you may wish to discontinue using. By avoiding these terms and selecting more inclusive ways to show respect, you are on the road to building bridges to understanding and an environment conducive to more effective team work and one-on-one relations with others.

Religion

I never want to hear...
—I can't have fun, because I am religious.
—I can't think for myself, I must check with the church, Pope, etc.
—I should stop referring to God when at work.
—I am constantly trying to recruit or convert others.
—All born-again Christians are self-righteous and narrow-minded.

I never want to see...
—another church being burned due to hatred.
—another war fought under the shield of religion.

I never want to experience...
—discrimination due to religious or spiritual beliefs.
—one religion judging another as "not as good as."

Sexual Orientation

I never want to see ...

—someone "out" a homosexual. It is up to the individual to decide with whom to discuss sexuality.

—a straight man imitate a gay man by making hand and wrist gestures.

I never want to hear...

—"Don't ask, don't tell."

—"Don't be so political!"

—that homosexuality is a choice—it is not. Do heterosexuals choose to be straight?

—it just takes the "right" heterosexual to make a gay or lesbian straight.

—"You just haven't found the right man or woman yet."

—gay men are feminine and lesbian women are "butch."

—"What a waste!" when referring to homosexuals.

—a person's sexual orientation used as part of the description of the person.

—heterosexual persons say that homosexual persons are sexually interested in them just because they are of the same gender. (We can appreciate the attractiveness of a person without it being sexual, just as heterosexuals can recognize attractive homosexual or heterosexuals, without being sexually attracted to them.)

—someone trying to find out why someone "turned" gay. (We just are.)

—the words "faggot", "fag", "bull-dike", "butch", or "fem".

—others say, "Just don't flaunt it." (Straights flaunt their sexuality all the time.)

I never want to experience ...

—being asked who the "husband" in the relationship is.

—someone saying to me, "Gee, you don't look gay."

—being afraid to walk down the street, or participate in gay pride events, for fear of being attacked.

African American

I never want to see ...

—people grab their purse tighter, just because a Black man is walking in their direction.

—police brutality or harassment toward people just because of the color of their skin.

—bi-racial couples being stared at or verbally abused.

—African American children being abused by teachers, for example, writing on their face with permanent markers.

I never want to hear ...

—"There goes the neighborhood."

—"You don't sound Black!"

—"We are in the 'wrong' neighborhood,'" when driving a nice car or just walking down the street.

—that a multi-ethnic child was told her existence was a mistake.

—comments that African Americans are lazy and on welfare.

—African American men are irresponsible.

—"Go back to Africa, where you came from." I was born in the United States.

—comments that all African Americans come from the ghetto.

—African Americans are not patriotic.

—all African American young men are gang bangers.

—"I know how she or he got her or his job."

Hispanic/Mexican

I never want to see ...

—the Mexican tourist trinket of a man sleeping at the foot of a tree. We are hard workers. This symbolizes laziness.

—the term *Hispanic*. I am Mexican and proud of it.

—Hispanic laborers being mistreated.

I never want to hear ...

—the term *wetbacks.*

—"Are you legal?"

—"Don't speak Spanish at work." We are often discussing work.

I never want to experience ...

—being harassed by police.

—feeling ashamed because I speak Spanish.

American Indian

I never want to hear ...

—the word *squaw.* It is not an Indian word, and it is very derogatory.

—we are too sensitive. Get over it.

—that all Native Americans are drunks and live on reservations.

—"You can't do that! This is a hospital!" (when practicing healing rituals).

I never want to see ...

—our ancestral artifacts stolen or treated with disrespect.

—derogatory caricatures of American Indians as sports team mascots.

—non-Indians acting as though they are in movies.

Asian

I never want to hear ...

—"Asian." Take the time to ask which nationality to which you are referring.

—all Asians are terrible drivers.

—all Asians are smart.

—"Jap."

—"Go back to your country." Many of our ancestors helped build the United States.

I never want to see ...

—others making fun of the shape of our eyes.

European American

I never want to hear ...

—your problems are my fault.

—"You just don't get it."

—"All Whites are bigots."

I never want to see ...

—discrimination towards anyone, regardless of race.

—people burning the flag.

I never want to experience ...

—loss of our freedoms.

People with Disabilities

I never want to hear ...

—"You can't ..."

—"Handicapped."

I never want to see ...

—people with disabilities being stared at.

—people making fun of us.

I never want to experience ...

—job discrimination.

—not being able to get on a bus due to lack of proper equipment on the bus.

—being talked at as though I am not present.

Women

I never want to hear ...

—"When are you going to have a baby?"

—"When are you going to get married?"

—women are the weaker sex.

—we are poor money managers.

—"I know why you got that job."

I never want to see ...

—women or girls being verbally or physically abused.

—women "killing" themselves to be thin.

—women being passed over for certain jobs because they
are not pretty enough.

I never want to experience ...
—discrimination.
—domestic abuse.
—less than equal pay for equal work.

Men

I never want to hear ...
—all men are pigs.
—men are insensitive.
—"You've got it so easy."

I never want to see ...
—men harassing anyone.
—men being passed over because of Affirmative Action.

Making a Difference

**Form a small group of collegues to explore the stereotyp-
ical thinking causes. Have each member share the following information:**

- Describe a time in your childhood when you didn't fit
  in. What was the situation; how did you feel; how did
  you react?
- Discuss the comments listed on the previous pages.
  For the groups of which you are a member, share what
  you never want to see, hear or experience.
- Record your key learnings and insights as a result of
  this exercise.

_____

_____

_____

_____

_____

_____

14

What Are the Habits of Managers Who Create and Sustain an Environment That Supports Diversity?

"The furthest place on earth to journey is into the presence of the person nearest you."
—Nelle Morton

Think of a leader/manager in your life who really motivated you to be the best you could be. What attributes or characteristics describe him or her? What habits did he or she have that worked for you? Over the past two years, I have asked hundreds of managers that question. Here is a sampling of the most frequent answers.

He or she:

- Was fair and respectful toward others.
- Had high personal standards.
- Believed in my abilities and potential.
- Helped me believe in myself.
- Encouraged and stretched me.
- Led by example.
- Mentored and coached.
- Asked for and appreciated different points of view.
- Listened.
- Criticized objectively.
- Had integrity; was honorable.
- Helped me solve my own problems.
- Had a vision.
- Developed a trusting environment.

The specific word, *diversity*, was rarely used when people described their best, favorite, or most effective manager. However, *fairness*, *respect*, *objectiveness*, and *listening* recurred frequently.

These attributes describe an effective manager and leader. The key within a diverse environment is to be able to practice these behaviors with *all* workers, rather than only employees with whom you are most comfortable. Developing the diversity dimension of leadership requires a commitment to demonstrate the following behaviors on a regular basis:

• **Learn each individual's professional aspirations and support their efforts to reach them.** Many organizations have some type of career development or succession planning process. In order to make these programs more effective within a diverse environment, be sure that you are talking to all of your staff about their career aspirations. Even if your organization does not have many opportunities for individuals looking for upward mobility, your interest in their career and your assistance in their development will be greatly appreciated and usually motivates people to do their best work. If there are no opportunities within the organization and the employee ultimately leaves the company, the company then has a positive ambassador in the overall community.

- **Create opportunities for highly talented employees to be exposed to leaders who may not otherwise interact with them.** Create opportunities where they present a report, attend a meeting in your place, or do various other things whereby they can interact with leaders in the organization who, if impressed, can impact their career in a positive way.

- **Create cross-functional teams.** As organizations have downsized, right-sized, and re-engineered their businesses, many management positions have been eliminated, thus requiring groups to work together as teams in order to complete the necessary tasks. When you create cross-functional teams, ideas flourish. People are exposed to each other and discover that different departments have different viewpoints, and that is beneficial to the overall innovation potential of the organization. When creating these teams, remember that putting people together does not automatically make them a team. Attention does need to be given to developing that group of people into an effective, trusting team.

- **Volunteer for community projects that teach tolerance, both directly and indirectly.** By doing this, you set the example that you are continually enhancing your understanding and appreciation of people different than you. That behavior can encourage others within the organization to do the same. For example, you may choose to become a mentor within the Big Brothers/Big Sisters organization. This can enable you to better understand young people. The experience can teach tolerance and patience, and it can certainly will help you appreciate what is important to people whose backgrounds may be different than yours. These learnings have great application once you are then at work, interacting with your staff day to day.

- **Delegate fairly.** Sometimes we have a tendency to delegate to the same people all the time because they do good work and we know things will be done well. However, if we are going to truly develop each staff member, regardless of their packaging, we need to identify projects, tasks, and responsibilities that could further develop their skills. Once the task is delegated, be sure to coach and counsel, and be clear regarding your expectations and the results.

- **Communicate and support intolerance of inappropriate and disrespectful behavior.** This must be an ongoing activity, one where you are constantly looking for opportunities to teach tolerance and respect within the workplace.

- **Evaluate performance objectively.** Employees really want to do a good job. The problem is often they don't know what a good job is, because the clues from management and leadership are unclear. As soon as a person joins an organization, she or he should be given a clear job description, and the specific goals and objectives for that individual should be developed. The criteria for measurement should be clarified. Throughout the evaluation period, feedback should be given so that when the evaluation review is actually conducted, neither the manager nor the employees is surprised by the results. It is not easy being totally objective all the time. However, if the skills and expectations for the job are clear, the measurement criteria is clear, and the feedback is continuous, then it becomes easier for you to be fair with each employee.

- **Consider individual needs when enforcing company policies and guidelines.** The idea is to be fair. However, "fair" does not necessarily mean "the same." There are times when you have to decide how to implement policies without showing favoritism while recognizing differences. An example might be with work schedules. Although within a department, and within the same job category, everyone is probably expected to arrive at the same time and leave at the same time, it would be appropriate, when necessary, to allow flex-time as long as it is clear that the total amount of time required for work is covered. Job sharing is also helpful here. If parents have child-related issues, effective managers consider those issues and determine whether or not exceptions are necessary while balancing the effect of making those exceptions and their impact on the overall department. Not an easy thing to do. Rather than try to come up with the best idea alone, solicit input from the employees involved and from other managers to determine what the most appropriate action is.

You may have noticed that nowhere in this chapter have I mentioned doing things based on ethnicity, gender, disability, age, and the like. It is critical that effective leaders and managers realize that everyone in the organization contributes to its diversity. The more you are able to connect with individuals, the more you will be able to create an environment that causes them to produce at their highest level, regardless of their packaging.

Making a Difference

1. **Make time to talk privately with each of your employees on a regular basis.** For example, if you have 10 employees, provide each with 30 minutes every two weeks where they have the opportunity to share with you what-

ever they wish. They can ask any questions, give you ideas, and you have the opportunity to get to know them personally and coach and counsel them as necessary.

2. **Ask your staff, individually, how they would prefer to be managed and how they would prefer to be rewarded.** Often we assume money is what everyone wants. This is not necessarily true. Using learning assessments such as the Personal Profile or other tools to better understand communications styles and ingredients for the most motivating environments for different styles can be very helpful for both you and the employee. When you ask an employee how he or she wishes to be rewarded, you may discover personal interests, and professional aspirations that you can be supportive of. For example, perhaps one employee might be most motivated by having the company pay part of his or her child's tuition. A child free person may be most appreciative if the company provided additional vacation time so that she or he could visit a favorite place.

3. **Take your staff to lunch every now and then, just to chat.** The more actions you take to demonstrate sincere interest in the individual, the more likely your staff will want to "go the extra mile." The challenge is to be able to make the time. However, once you do, you will be more likely to see the real person, instead of just their "packaging." Their differences will then be an asset instead of a barrier.

15

As a Manager, I'm Held Accountable for Cost. I Can't Afford to Hire the Disabled, Can I?

> "All people have something to contribute to society. It's not what a person doesn't have, it's what he or she does have to offer that's important."
> —*What Everybody Should Know About Disabilities*

One of the myths that surround people with disabilities is that the employing organization has to take extraordinary and costly measures to accommodate their needs in the workplace. This is truly a myth. Many people with disabilities require no special adjustments and others require very few. The problem is that hiring managers allow their fears, discomforts, and biases to get in the way of making objective decisions about the skills, talents, and abilities of a person with a major disability.

Not hiring people with disabilities is costly. In 1992, The President's Committee on Employment of People with Disabilities conducted a study that indicated that, at that time, there were 20 million people with disabilities who were of working age (16 to 65). Of those 20 million, 14 million wanted to work. Of that 14 million, 9 million were unemployed. Although the Americans with Disabilities Act makes it illegal to discriminate against a person with disabilities, the practice still goes on. Biases and stereotypes get in the way just as it does with other people with visible differences.

Over the past 20 years, I have made presentations to and conducted training for thousands of people. To this day, I still can count only a very few participants who were in my audience, employed by my clients, who happened to have disabilities. Corporations, and society in general, are not intentionally biased. However, we fear that which we don't know, and we rely on myths when we have no factual information. Without the facts, people assume that a person with disabilities simply cannot do certain jobs. Yet all of us have seen individuals on television, and some of us have experienced firsthand, people who have disabilities performing the same types of jobs that able-bodied people do.

As a professional speaker, and performance consultant, I am required to travel extensively, to speak to groups, to use AV equipment, and so on. Within my profession alone, there are many people who happen to have disabilities who do the same things I do. There are several keynote speakers who are blind, who use a wheelchair, and who have hearing impairments or other disabilities. The limitations are only in the mind of the uninformed.

The question of cost is an interesting one because, in fact, it costs more money *not* to employ people with disabilities. Certainly, those 9 million, who are not employed even though they want to work, still have to eat and sleep. Without employment, many must rely on public assistance. The government supports public assistance. The government is paid for by "we, the people." Wouldn't it make more sense to provide more opportunities for individuals who happen to have a disability to be gainfully employed?

Going beyond one's biases is not easy in this case. It requires accepting that we have biases. I worked for a car dealership for a short period of time, and to the amazement of many, one of the sales consultants was a person who used a wheelchair. Most sales managers would argue, when I would share this story during presentations, that this individual could not perform a very important step in the sales process, which is conducting the demonstration drive. Because of that assumption, many times he was turned down for automotive sales positions.

One of the problems is that hiring managers rarely ask candidates how they would perform a required step in the job that appears to be one that they would not be able to do. Managers assume that "reasonable accommodations" require thousands and thousands of dollars.

In this case, the dealership did not have to spend any money at all. Since this particular sales department was set up as teams, the team worked out the details of how best to satisfy the requirement of taking all customers on a demo drive, even though it would be impractical to fit each car for handicapped accessibility. In other words, when Pat reached that step in the sales process, he would T.O., as it's said in the business (turnover), his customer to one of his team members who would accompany the customer. When the customer and the team member returned to the dealership, Pat would resume the negotiation process. Internal to the dealership, this is a critical step in the sales process. This is the time when the sales consultant begins to really determine if the customer loves this car, is ready to buy, or perhaps, should be shown other alternatives. Obviously, Pat would not be able to see those signals, but his team member could. Had Pat chosen to sue the dealerships that turned him down, the courts would probably see this step simply as an internal detail that could be worked out, rather than a clear job requirement that could not be performed by a person in a wheelchair. Not only was Pat able to perform his job, he was often Salesperson of the Month.

While conducting a diversity workshop, I was thrilled to have, as a participant, an individual who was completely deaf. Many times during keynote presentations, I had people with hearing disabilities in the audience, but I had never had the experience of such a participant in a training session, which had many small group discussions, team activities, and the like. Two interpreters accompanied this participant for the entire seven-hour program and signed everything. It was fascinating to watch the other participants' reaction to having the individual in class. I thought, "My, this organization is progressive," because they had employed this individual for 15 years. Unfortunately, however, his perspective was different.

"They never ask me about my career aspirations. They assume I can only do the specific job they originally hired me for. They complain when I do the same things other employees do, like attend training, because it costs them money. [In this organization, all employees are required to receive 40 hours of training per year.] When I attend training classes, they must employ two interpreters, which cost $50 per hour, each. They never seem to realize that my participation in these seminars improves my skills and abilities, enables me to interact with others, just like any other employee. If they didn't complain so much, it would boost my motivation and perhaps

I'd be even more productive when I go back to work."

Another client is a customer service center. The employees answer a 1-800 line to process the repair claims for customers of a particular appliance. Since the responsibilities require workers to sit at a computer terminal, being ambulatory by foot is not required. The organization regularly works with habilitation centers around the city to identify individuals with the skills to perform these duties. One would think this would be a great job for some people who use wheelchairs.

The organization's challenge is not finding people who can do the job, rather it is getting them to the job. In most communities today, public buses have lifts for people who need them. However, most people who use wheelchairs have told me that the lifts frequently do not work, or there is insufficient funding to equip enough buses to accommodate their needs. One individual told me he had to wait two hours before a bus finally had a lift that worked. Imagine if you could not predict what time you would arrive at work because the transportation you required frequently was non-operational. Some of you would say, "Well, they should purchase a car that can accommodate their needs." That proposition is extremely expensive and if the person is not employed, from where will the money come?

Because people are so uncomfortable around others who are different in this way, people show their discomfort in amusing, and sometimes annoying, ways. Have you ever talked louder when speaking to a blind person as though that would help him or her see you? Have you ever "helped" a person in a wheelchair without asking her or him first? Often, I am told, people will try to help and then become angered when the person with the disability says, "No, thank you." Perhaps we should put ourselves in their position. If a person uses a wheelchair, most likely he or she knows how to manipulate it correctly. So, the reason the person with the disability may say, "No, thank you" could be stemming from safety issues. Perhaps it is in fact, easier for them to simply do things for themselves rather than watching us trip over ourselves trying to be helpful.

The government has been an excellent example of how to be insensitive when dealing with people with disabilities. The word *handicapped* is stamped all over the place. Yet, most people know that using that particular word is not favored. Perhaps understanding the reason would be helpful in motivating people to avoid such a word. *Handicapped* originated from the British term that identified people who could legally beg for money in public, centuries ago. If persons were disabled, they could legally beg for money in public by holding a cap in hand. Thus, the word *handicapped* implies that people with disabilities are begging. Certainly, they are not. Just like others with differences, they are simply requesting an opportunity to utilize their skills, abilities, and talents regardless of their packaging.

Organizations such as the Holiday Inn and McDonalds have been recognized over the past several years for their efforts to employ people with disabilities, both physical and developmental. As we approach the year 2000 the labor pool continues to shrink, yet, higher skill levels are needed. Wouldn't it make sense that employing organizations more clearly and objectively identify the skills and abilities needed and hire people who can perform those skills regardless of their packaging?

Salt River Project, a utility company in Arizona, works closely with the habilitation center to employ people who are physically or developmentally disabled in their reclamation efforts. The Salt River Project salvages as much wasted material as possible to reduce the cost of utilities and to save the environment. Since working in cooperation with the habilitation center, they have realized two things: the employees are thrilled to have the opportunity to work productively, and the employees of SRP continually raise their level of awareness and understanding of the many skills and talents of all individuals. Creating work opportunities for people with disabilities is not just the right thing to do, it is the economic thing to do.

Making a Difference

There are several actions you can take to raise your level of understanding and acceptance of people with disabilities. Try these suggestions and record your reactions.

1. **Wear a blindfold for an hour or two and have a friend or colleague lead you around the workplace.** Afterwards, record your reactions. Were you trusting? Were you fearful? Were there many hazards?

   _____

   _____

   _____

2. **Rent a wheelchair and then go to a shopping mall.** Notice how people react to you. Do they look at you when they speak or do they look at a friend who is accompanying you most of the time? How easy or difficult is it to get around? Try using the rest room.

   _____

   _____

   _____

3. **Place a telephone call using a specially equipped phone for people with hearing impairments (TDD).**

   _____

   _____

   _____

4. **Become a volunteer for community organizations that provide services to people with disabilities, such as cerebral palsy or multiple sclerosis. Record your reactions and learnings.**

   _____

   _____

   _____

16

How Can I Stop Inappropriate Behavior in the Workplace and Yet Maintain My Relationships with Others?

"When different talents and ideas rub up against each other, there is friction, yes. But also sparks, fire, light and—eventually—brilliance!"
—Nancy O'Neill

I believe one of the major reasons people do not speak up more often when they observe inappropriate behavior is because they do not know how to speak up when they have to deal with the offender on a regular basis. It is easier just to be silent. That silence, however, perpetuates inappropriate behavior. Each of us, if we really choose to make a difference, must be unwilling to be a part of the silent majority on this issue. The following is a four-step process for giving feedback that is easy to understand but takes practice to implement easily. The process is called **S.T.O.P.**

S—State the inappropriate behavior objectively.

When beginning this feedback, describe the specific behavior that needs to be changed in an objective, unemotional way. Too often when we do speak up regarding inappropriate behavior we are emotional, we show our anger, and we start with feelings. Many times, all of the above causes the offender to become defensive or to go into denial. In order to maintain your objectivity and to assure that the offender clearly understands what you are referring to, simply state what he or she has done.

T—Tell the offender how you feel when she or he performs this inappropriate behavior.

You may state feelings or opinions. Feelings really work best. Does it make you angry? Hurt? Excluded? Offended? Be careful not to judge; simply state how you react to this behavior.

O—Options, options, options.

Provide alternative behavioral suggestions. Frequently, when we tell others to stop doing something, we don't tell them what we would prefer instead.

P—Positive results.

Share with the offender what would be in it for her or him if he or she chooses to change behavior. Each of us behaves based on "what's in it for me." It is important that you answer this question. Change does not occur unless there is a reason. If the individual cannot see a good reason to change behavior, the inappropriate behavior usually continues. If the inappropriate behavior also breaks company policy, the consequences, should the person choose not to change his or her behavior, could be a disciplinary one by the company. However, as often as possible when using this technique, try not to threaten the person at this step. Rather, show positive, interpersonal relationship results should he or she choose to change his or her behavior.

Several years ago, after having taught this technique many times, I was faced with a personal situation where I had to walk my talk. A very close friend had the habit of using the term *faggot* often. Whenever he was referring to someone he did not like or someone who showed effeminate behavior, he would use this label. I find the term very offensive so I realized I needed to use the S.T.O.P. technique. Just like most people, initially I was hesitant. This individual was, and today still is, a very dear friend. I did not want to offend him or create any situation that would interfere with our friendship. He and his girlfriend were among six of us that often socialized together; my husband and I, he and his girlfriend, and another couple. Let's call him Walter.

While the six of us were enjoying a sunny and hot weekend afternoon in Phoenix, Walter used the word. I had informed my husband earlier that if Walter used that term again, I would need to speak with him. I did not want my husband to be surprised nor caught off guard should things not go well. I waited for Walter to be in a situation where he and I could talk privately. Eventually, when he entered the kitchen to help himself to refreshments, I followed him. This technique only takes about 45 seconds. It is not intended that the offender respond at that time. What is important is that you get your points across quickly, non-judgmentally, and clearly. Here's what happened.

"Walter, when you use the word 'faggot' [step one—S] it offends me and makes me very uncomfortable in your presence [step two—T]. I would prefer that, if you must use a descriptor of this kind, you use words that are more appropriate, such as homosexual, gay, lesbian, etc. Actually, I would prefer that you not use a term at all unless you know, for a fact, that the individual happens to be homosexual and that piece of information is pertinent to the story you are sharing with us at the time [step three—O]. If you are willing to change your behavior in this way, at least in my presence, you certainly will be more welcome in our home [step four—P]. This invisible barrier that has come up between us will dissipate, and you, then, can tell your wonderful stories without any concern of offending me or anyone else in the group."

Walter responded by not responding at all. He had a stunned look on his face. He walked away, went back outside, and dove into the pool. I thought, "Oh well. No change here." However, I was wrong.

Shortly thereafter when he and his girlfriend and the other couple went out to dinner, he shared this experience with them. It was not complimentary to me. Apparently, however, no one took his side even though I had not shared with anyone what I had done. Although they didn't criticize him, they didn't support the labels that he was, at least momentarily, putting on me. I learned of this interaction from one of the four other individuals.

The next several times that Walter and I were in each other's company, I noticed that he did not use that term. I made it a point to let him know that I noticed his changed behavior and how much I appreciated it. I did this in private. Several months later, when chatting with one of the other members of this party of friends, I was told that Walter no longer used the term in their presence either. A few years later, I was talking to another member of this group about diversity training in general. This member works for an organization that has many diversity initiatives in place and I'm always interested in learning what they are doing. Her husband works with Walter. She told me, and I later confirmed it with her husband, that indeed, Walter no longer used this term at work.

The point is this; the feedback took approximately 45 seconds. My objective was to get Walter to stop using that word, at least in my presence. I exceeded my objective and change occurred. I cannot guarantee that every time you use this process you will have similar results. However, you will never know the impact you, as one individual, can have on another individual unless you try.

Making a Difference

The best way to utilize this technique is to initially use it in a non-threatening environment.

1. **Use the S.T.O.P. technique when giving feedback** to a child regarding any type of inappropriate behavior. Once you have gotten comfortable with the process, then attempt it with others.

2. **Plan what you will say ahead of time.** Writing it out might be helpful so that you can focus your thoughts, stay objective, and identify options.

3. **Be sure you're in a private place when you walk through these steps.** If the offender does become defensive or goes into denial, simply repeat the process calmly.

4. **Be sure to recognize and show appreciation** for changed behavior as quickly as possible so that others know this was, and is, important to you and that you appreciate their efforts.

17

Can One Person Make a Difference?

> "Either we are pulling together or we are pulling apart. There's really no in-between."
> —Kobi Yamada

As we analyze the many challenges present in our society when interacting with the many differences among us all, it can sometimes seem overwhelming. It can seem as though one person cannot make a difference. I believe that each of us, individually, can make a tremendous difference.

No major social change has ever occurred because the masses, all of a sudden, decided it was a good thing to do. Consider the works of Gandhi, Martin Luther King Jr., Jesus, and Nelson Mandela, Lech Walesa, and others. Each of them had a strong belief and commitment. Each of them was able to make major changes. You, too, in your own way, can change your community, your workplace, and the overall respect and acceptance of people on this planet.

In order to continue this journey of valuing diversity, you need three things. You already possess all three.

Each of us has a sub-conscious behavior guide. It is represented by the inner voice that is constantly telling us what to do and what to believe.

The first level—*The Protector*—represents our mask or façade. We use it when we most want to be accepted. It tells us to act this way or that, depending on what will be accepted by those around us at the time. We all must wear a façade sometime, in order to fit in. Some people are forced to wear this mask, even when they would rather not, because those in power make rules for those who are not. The rules are often based on what makes them comfortable, not what makes the most sense or what is most respectful of individuals. For example, many men and women wear suits to work, not because they really want to, but because their work culture dictates that suits will enable them to be taken seriously and look like they have potential. There is nothing wrong with wearing suits. However, clothes do not, by themselves indicate a person's ability to get the job done well. Because wearing something other than a suit would be risky, many people just follow the norm.

The second level is *The Judge.* When we are at this level we are motivated to be right. This is the most dangerous of the three because most people rarely examine the messages here. They therefore act without thought. Values and beliefs reside here, along with biases, stereotypes, and prejudice. Unexamined, these messages affect how we treat others, and what we believe about others. Our motivation at this level is to be right. Do you know someone who must be right all the time? They are stuck at the Judge level. We depend on this level most often when we are afraid or stressed. At work, if you are afraid of what your superiors think of you, or are afraid of losing your job to downsizing, rightsizing, or other euphemistic terms for firing people, you might be reacting to messages at this level. We don't think of all the stereotypes at once, only the ones we need. Many of the previous stories in this book demonstrate how we use the information at this level.

Although we need beliefs and values, we need to examine them once in a while to determine whether they still fit. For example, many people were taught as children to "clean their plate, eat all their food." Perhaps if more adults would realize that message no longer is necessary, there would be fewer people on diets. The value we were supposed to learn was not to waste. We learned it through a behavior that is no longer needed to maintain the value. All of our values and beliefs are connected to behaviors.

When we are so focused on being right, we lose the willingness to understand others and appreciate different ways of thinking and behaving.

The third level is *The Authenticator.* Our motivation is just "to be". Unfortunately, as adults we are not at this level much because we are so busy judging or worrying about being judged. At this level we are willing to accept others regardless of their packaging. We evaluate situations and people based on facts, instead of relying on stereotypes. Children tend to be at this level until they learn the messages that adults pass on to them. This is the level that truly is able to value the diversity of people without judging.

The Subconscious Behavior Guide

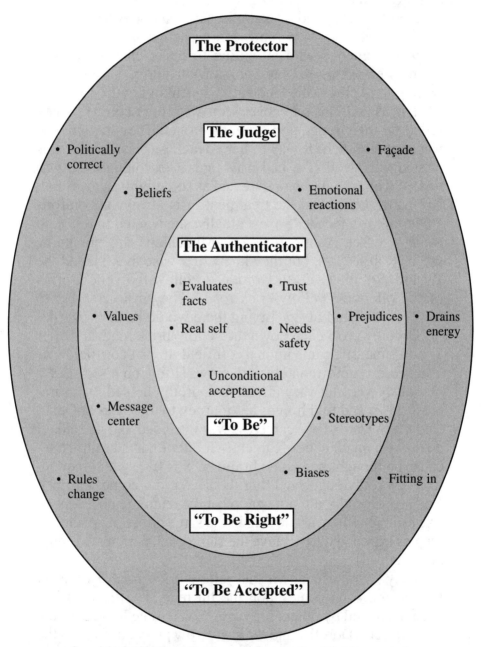

Let me demonstrate how the model works through an analogy of the *Wizard of Oz.*

Dorothy was tired of being in Kansas. She wanted to explore. Dorothy actually represents a change agent. A change agent is someone who is willing to make change happen, often by exploring new and unknown territory. Dorothy was willing to explore. She landed in Munchkin Land.

The Munchkins had never seen a Dorothy before so they relied on their Judge and stereotyped her. They thought she was a good witch. It was to her advantage because she was treated very well, she had privilege. Even though she was treated well, she was being treated as something she was not. No matter how good the treatment, it is always uncomfortable to wear a facade. So, eventually, she wanted to return to Kansas to see Auntie Em. The Munchkins did not know where Kansas was, but they knew of a wise man named the Wizard. So, they said to Dorothy, "Follow the yellow-brick road. Follow the yellow-brick road." They instructed her to look for the Land of Oz. Living there would be the Wizard.

Dorothy proceeded down the yellow-brick road, and after a short time, she came upon a cornfield. In that cornfield was a scarecrow, unfortunately with crows sitting on his arms. He obviously was not very effective. Dorothy helped the scarecrow down and told him of her journey to the Land of Oz, to find the Wizard. The scarecrow was intrigued and he said, "I could be a much better scarecrow if only I had a brain!" (Because he thought he had no brain, he was flimsy and ineffective.) Dorothy suggested that the scarecrow come with her. You see, Dorothy did not care what the team member looked like as long as he was moving in the same direction as she. As long as he wanted to achieve the same goal, perhaps he could be of help.

They continued down the yellow-brick road a little bit farther and soon came upon the tin man. The tin man had been neglected by others for years. You see, he looked a little too different. Dorothy and the scarecrow proceeded to tell the tin man about the Land of Oz and this man called the Wizard. The tin man then said, "I would be a much better tin man if only I had a heart." (Perhaps his rigidity was due to his perceived lack of heart.) Dorothy said, "The Wizard, Oz. Come on with us." They proceeded down the yellow-brick road.

They eventually came upon a forest and the trees were rattling. From behind the trees jumped the cowardly lion. They told the cowardly lion their story, and the lion said, "I would be king of the jungle if only I had courage!" (Because he did not follow his own convictions, he was intimidated by anyone who did, thus always a follower.) Dorothy invited the lion to join their team and find the Wizard in the Land of Oz.

So the four of them, plus Toto, trekked through many perils and eventually arrived at Emerald City. They knocked on the door. As powerful as the Wizard was, he too did not believe he would be accepted just as he was. He too wore a mask, his Protector. He was a very smart man, however. He knew that if he told them they had a brain, a heart, and courage, they would not believe him. They had to experience it.

Just as you have begun to experience the journey of valuing diversity. You could have watched a videotape, or just read one or two chapters of this book. Diversity, however, has to be experienced to be understood so your journey has just begun.

The Wizard informed Dorothy, the scarecrow, the tin man, and the lion that they would need to get the broom of the wicked witch, (she represents the obstacles in our lives) and he sent them off on their task. They used their brain, heart, and courage, and came back with the broom. It took Toto, the dog, (The Authenticator) to discover the real Wizard. Toto, you see, represents the innocence and truthfulness of children. Hate has to be carefully taught. Children begin their lives without judgment and ask questions to seek the truth. He represents unconditional acceptance.

The Wizard informed them that they had a brain, a heart,

and courage all the time. Here's how these three ingredients relate to you.

You have a brain. Certainly, you had that before you began to read this book. A brain alone, however, is not enough, because a brain alone looks for the most efficient answers to puzzles. The most efficient answers are often stereotypical and biased. They are quick but incorrect. Just using our brain can lead us, ultimately, to tyranny because it will rely on the messages within the judge. A brain by itself wants to be right, and if I am right, that makes you wrong, which immediately begins a conflict.

So you must connect your brain to your heart. By doing so, you will be empowered to become more patient, to be willing to listen to other points of view, to be less fearful of the unknown, and to be more willing to understand.

A brain and a heart alone are still not quite enough because they do not move you to action. Of the three, courage is the most important. By using your courage, you will be more willing to ask questions, more capable of speaking up against inappropriate behavior and wrongful actions, more determined to have a voice rather than following the silent majority.

I encourage you to use your courage to make a difference, one person at a time.

Afterword

IT'S NOT REALLY ME

It is not me who speaks
when my words are truly stirring,
It is Mother Father God who speak through me.

It is not me who is Lion-Hearted
when someone sheds a tear
because they are deeply moved
It is Mother Father God using me as their vehicle
to make a difference.

I am on a never-ending journey
to somehow make a difference.
When I do
It is really Mother Father God
choosing this messenger
to create the environment for little miracles.

Thank you for allowing me to share,

Lenora

Appendix

The Cold Within

Six humans trapped by happenstance
In black and bitter cold
Each one possessed a stick of wood,
Or so the story's told.

Their dying fire in need of logs,
The first woman held hers back,
For the faces around the fire
She noticed one of them was black.

The next man looking cross the way
Saw one not of his church,
And couldn't bring himself to give
The first stick of birch.

The third one sat in tattered clothes
He gave his coat a hitch.
Why should his log be put in use
To warm the idle rich?

The rich man just sat back and thought
Of the wealth he had in store,
And how to keep what he had earned
From the lazy, shiftless poor.

The black man's face bespoke revenge
As the fire passed from his sight.
For all he saw in his stick of wood
Was a chance to spite the white.

And the last man of this forlorn group
Did naught except for gain.
Giving only to those who gave
Was how he played the game.

The logs held tight in death's still hands
Was proof of human sin.
They didn't die from the cold without
They died from the cold within.

—Author Unknown

(Printed with permission from Carlson Learning Company,
1998)

Celebrate You

You are worth celebrating.
You are worth celebrating.
You are unique.

In all the world, there is only one you.
There is only one person with your talents,
Your experience, your gift.
No one can take your place!
God created only one of you, precious in His sight.
You have immense potential to love, to care,
to create, to grow, to sacrifice,
if you believe in yourself.
It doesn't matter your age, your color,
Or whether your parents loved you or not.
(Maybe they wanted to, but didn't know how.)
Let that go, it belongs to the past; you belong to the now.
It doesn't matter what you've been, the wrong you've done,
The mistakes you've made, the people you've hurt. You are
forgiven. You are accepted, you're OK.

Celebrate you.

Begin now. Start now. Give yourself a new birth. Today.
You are you, and that is all you need to be.
You are temporary. Here today and gone tomorrow.
But today, today can be a new beginning, a new thing, a
new life.
You deserve this new life, it is given freely.
That is the miracle called God.
So celebrate the miracle and celebrate you!

—Clyde Reid
(Printed with permission from Humor Consultants, Inc.,
1998)

Bibliography and Reference List

Carr-Ruffino, Norma. *Managing Diversity: People Skills for a Multicultural Workplace.* New York: International Thomson, 1996.

Cox, Taylor, Jr. *Cultural Diversity in Organizations: Theory, Research and Practice.* San Francisco: Berrett-Koehler, 1993.

D'Amico, Carol, and Richard W. Judy. *Workforce 2020.* Hudson Institute, 1997.

Fernandez, John P. *Managing a Diverse Work Force: Regaining the Competitive Edge.* Lexington, Mass.: Lexington Books, 1991.

Gentile, Mary C. *Differences That Work: Organizational Excellence through Diversity.* Boston: Harvard Business School Press, 1994.

Hayles, Robert, and Armida Russell. *The Diversity Directive.* New York: McGraw Hill, 1997.

Hateley, Barbara, and Warren H. Schmidt. *A Peacock in the Land of Penguins: A Tale of Diversity and Discovery.* San Francisco: Berrett-Koehler, 1995.

Helminiak, Daniel A. *What the Bible Really Says About Homosexuality.* San Francisco: Alamo Square Press, 1995.

Johnston, William B., and Arnold H. Packer. *Workforce 2000.* New York: Hudson Institute, 1987.

Powers, Bob, and Alan Ellis. *A Manager's Guide to Sexual Orientation in the Workplace.* New York: Routledge, 1995.

Thomas, R. Roosevelt , Jr. *Beyond Race and Gender.* American Management Association, 1991.

Thiederman, Sondra. *Profiting in American's Multicultural Marketplace.* Lexington, Mass.: Lexington Books, 1991.

Diversity on the World Wide Web

1. National Association for Multicultural Education
   www.inform.umd.edu/CampusInfo/Committees/Assoc/NAME/

2. The EraM (Ethnicity, Racism and the Media) Program
   www.brad.ac.uk/research/eram/eram.htm

3. Webcult
   www.aguilade/sol.com/

4. Culture (Community)
   www.einet.net/galaxy/community/culture.htm.

5. Pathways to Diversity on the WWW
   www.usc.edu/Library/Q

6. Affirmative Action and Diversity Page
   http://humanitas.uscb.edu/aa.html

7. Clinton's Race Initiative
   www.pbs.org/news

8. Peto Projects
   www.owt.com/phs/classrooms/peto/stu.html

9. America's Stirfry: Home

   www.americas-stirfry.com/

10. Archives of Traditional Music

    www.indiana.edu/~libarchm/

11. Teaching Diversity

    www.cob.ohio_state.edu/~diversity/teach.htm

12. History of Indians in the U.S

    http://calvin.cse.psu.edu/~gargi/India/A.History.of.Indians.in.the.USA

14. Ethnic Studies at USC

    http://www.usc.edu/Library/Ref/Ethnic

15. KIDPROJ's Multi-Cultural Calendar

    www.kidlink.org/KIDPROJMCC

16. Al-Hewar Website

    www.alhewan.com/ActionAlert.html

17. NAMES Project

    www.aidsquilt.org/

18. Open Dialog: Association of American Culture

    www.artswire.org/Artswire/taac/dialog/html

19. Gender & Race in the Media:LesBiGay and Gender & Race in Media: Cyberspace

    www.lib.iowa.edu/gw/comm/GenderMedia/gaymediahtml

20. Diversity

    http://latino.sscnet.ucla.edu/diversity1.html#AsA

21. The Anti-Racism Resources Home Page
   www.efn.org/~dennis_w/race.html

22. Indigenous People's Literature
   www.indians.org/natilt.html

23. Diversity in Business at Fisher College
   www.cob.ohio_state.edu/~diversity/

24. The Baha'I Faith Directory
   www.bcca.org/~cuoogt/

25. Equal Opportunity Publications (Career Center for Workforce Diversity)
   www.eop.com

26. Common Ground
   www.tulane.edu/~so_inst/

27. Amish Information
   www.800padutch.com/askamish.html

28. National Center for Research on Culture
   http://zzyx.ucsc.edu/cntr/entr.html

29. Voice of the Shuttle: Minority Studies Page
   http://humanites.ucsb.edu/shuttle/minority.html

30. San Francisco – City By the Bay
   www.kqed.org/from KQED/Cell/Calhist/intro.html

31. BEATS: Community & Society – PRIMER
   www.utne.com/primer/csprimer.html

32. Homeless in America
    www.commnet.edu/QVCTC/student/GaryOkeefe/homeless/frame2.html

33. Cornucopia of Disability Information
    http://codi.buffalo.edu/graph_based/

34. Welcome to the National Council on Disability (NCD)
    www.ncd.gov/

35. Anti-Defamation League
    www.adl.org/

36. Jewish Holidays of Passover (Pesach)
    www.melizo.com/holidays/passover

37. Hanukkah – Festival of Lights
    www.ort.org/ort/hanukkah/title.htm

38. Diversity Calendar '97
    www.jhu.edu/~hr1/vpadmin/diversity_calendar.html

39. Diversity Leadership Counsel
    www.peabody.jhu.edu/diversity/links.html

(If you know of other diversity sites, this author would be delighted to hear from you.)

Related Diversity Word Definitions

Affirmative Action

Proactive actions taken to provide equal opportunity, as in admission of employment, development, and promotions, for under-represented groups such as people of color, women, and people with special needs.

Assimilation

When the dominant group becomes the standard of behavior for all persons, and the majority expects members who are different to reject or repress their own culture and adopt the dominant culture in order to fit in. For example, in the past women were often expected to dress like men, *so as not to distract men* (the dominant group). Often rules are made simply for the comfort of the majority group rather than for clear business reasons.

Acculturation

A process used by organizations to help new members learn the values, customs, and norms of the organization. The goal is to focus the entire group on important organizational values without expecting those who are different to deny their own culture, while adapting to the organization's culture. For example, within many organizations men are allowed to have facial hair and wear an earring, and African

American women can wear braids without feeling as though they are "bucking the system."

Ageism
Biases, opinions, and beliefs about individuals based solely on their age (young or old).

Ableism
Fear or discomfort regarding people with special needs. Inappropriate comments and gestures about people who are disabled.

Bias
An inclination or preference, especially one that interferes with impartial judgment.

Bigot
A person fanatically devoted to one's own group, religion, politics, or ethnic group and intolerant of those who differ.

Homophobia
The fear of homosexuals. Making anti-gay jokes and gestures. Believing it is acceptable to treat gays and lesbians and others who are not heterosexual as less than equal human beings, and to expect them to follow strict rules of conduct not expected of heterosexuals.

Inclusion
The process of including all types of people in the group or team, by recognizing that differences are an asset for achieving high productivity.

Multiculturalism

That which pertains to, or is designed for, several individual cultures or groups (i.e., the United States Constitution). For example, Disney and AT&T now recognize homosexual couples as equal to married couples for the purpose of employee benefits and health care, rather than denying them benefits just because they are different.

Prejudice

An adverse opinion or judgment formed beforehand or without full knowledge or complete examination of the facts. Irrational hatred or suspicion of a specific group or religion.

Pluralism

A condition of society in which numerous distinct ethnic, religious, cultural, or age groups coexist.

Sexism

Prejudice or discrimination based on gender, especially against women. Arbitrary stereotyping of social roles based on gender.

Stereotypes

A conventional, usually oversimplified opinion, perception, or belief about a person; lacking in individuality.

Racism

The notion that one's own ethnic stock is superior. Prejudice or discrimination based on ethnicity.

Index

E

F

G

H

I

J